D1291322

THROUGH THE WINDOWS OF HEAVEN

100 Powerful Stories and Teachings from
Walter Martin, The Original Bible Answer Man

THROUGH THE WINDOWS OF HEAVEN

*100 Powerful Stories and Teachings from
Walter Martin, The Original Bible Answer Man*

Walter Martin
Jill Martin Rische

Nashville, Tennessee

© 1999 by Jill Martin Rische
All rights reserved
Printed in the United States of America

0-8054-2031-2

Published by Broadman & Holman Publishers,
Nashville, Tennessee
Typesetting: Leslie Joslin, Gray, Tennessee

Subject Heading: MEDITATIONS
Library of Congress Card Catalog Number: 99-14348

Unless otherwise noted, Scripture quotations are from the Holy
Bible, New International Version, copyright © 1973, 1978, 1984 by
International Bible Society.

Library of Congress Cataloging-in-Publication Data
Martin, Walter Ralston, 1928– .
    Through the windows of heaven / by Walter Martin and
Jill Martin Rische.
        p. cm.
    ISBN 0-8054-2031-2
    1. Meditations. I. Rische, Jill Martin, 1957– . II. Title.
BV4832.2.M316   1999
242—dc21
                                                        99-14348
                                                        CIP

1 2 3 4 5 — 03 02 01 00 99

To all the members of Walter Martin's Bible Class
down through the years—
You hold a special place in Dad's heart.
Keep bringing those Bibles!

And

To my husband, Kevin, and my daughter, Christina—
My happiness and my joy.

"I thank my God upon every remembrance of you."
—Philippians 1:3 KJV

Contents

We lay a fleece before you, Lord. Do something unusual. Open the windows of heaven and let us feel your power.

—Walter Martin

Preface

What can I say about my father, Dr. Walter Martin? He was a man, just like any other, with a man's strengths, weaknesses, and gifts. He was greatly loved by some and thoroughly hated by others. He was colorful, clever, tenacious, brilliant, and deeply dedicated to the cause of Christ. This combination of characteristics did not win him many popularity contests on earth, but I truly look forward to seeing his reward in heaven!

I will never forget the day he died. The phone rang about eight o'clock that Monday morning of June 26, 1989. I had been up late the night before due to a terrible thunderstorm, and I was very reluctant to answer it. The words my sister, Elaine, said to me were brief and devastating.

"Dad went to be with the Lord this morning, Jill."

I heard the words, but I couldn't believe them—I didn't want to believe them—yet they were terribly true; a painful reality that would forever change my life and the lives of my family.

How do you deal with the sudden, heartbreaking loss of a father? Someone you loved deeply, trusted implicitly, and respected so completely? To know he was gone for now—that it would be many years before I'd feel that big bear hug again—was an overwhelming grief.

But God was faithful; in the middle of all the pain and sorrow, he did keep his promise—he did comfort us. The love we felt from so many people comforted us, and I thank all of you for that love.

I would also like to thank Pastor Bradford of the Newport Mesa Christian Center in Costa Mesa, California, for his gracious consent in the use of the NMCC tapes. I am also deeply grateful to all those who continue to let us know how much Dad meant to them. "Pleasant words are a honeycomb, sweet to the soul and healing to the bones" (Prov. 16:24). Thank you for your wonderful encouragement!

Wherever possible, excerpts for this book were taken verbatim from the audiotapes, but some changes were made in certain instances where grammar and sentence structure needed revision. The original intent of the author was of paramount importance in the editing process.

This book is the result of many years of prayer. It is meant to strengthen and encourage you in your daily walk—but most of all it is meant to urge you to stand up for Jesus, as Dad did for more than forty years. Though he is gone, he still has a great deal to say and so much to teach. His ministry lives on through the work of *Walter Martin's* Religious InfoNet and the wonderful legacy of his tapes and books. I thank God for the opportunity to share them with you. I pray you will learn as much from them as I have over the past few years.

> "The LORD bless you
>   and keep you;
> the LORD make his face shine upon you
>   and be gracious to you;
> the LORD turn his face toward you
>   and give you peace.
>   —Numbers 6:24–26

Jill Martin Rische, 1999

1

Be a Champion!

Fight the good fight of the faith. Take hold of the eternal life to which you were called when you made your good confession in the presence of many witnesses.

—1 Timothy 6:12

A few years ago I became friends with Rocky Marciano, the undefeated heavyweight champion of the world. I met him at an airport, struck up a conversation, and we became friends. I witnessed to him, and we talked quite a bit. I learned to box when I was in school because I came from a rough neighborhood in Brooklyn where there were two kinds of people: the quick and the dead! If you weren't quick, you were dead. I'm a survivor, praise God! Marciano came from the same kind of neighborhood, so we had a lot in common.

One night, while eating a spaghetti dinner at three o'clock in the morning—I was his houseguest for the weekend—we were chatting about some of the problems of boxing, and I said to him, "You know, there was one thing that always bothered me about you, Rock. I could never figure it out. I've watched all the great fighters of the century, and I could never understand why you let yourself get hit so many times. You've been hit more times than any heavyweight champion in history. It looked like you were *begging for it!*"

He smiled and replied, "Good question. No one ever asked me that question before. I'm going to give you the answer. Stand up and square off with me."

"Oh, no," I said. "Crazy I might be—stupid, I'm not. No thanks!"

"We're not going to do anything," he laughed. "Just square off."

So we squared off. "OK," he said, "put out a left jab. Don't hit me, just put it out."

I stretched out my arm and lightly touched his chin with my fist. He said, "Now, watch."

He was in his cover-up style of boxing, the "peekaboo" style he was famous for, and he shot his left out at me as hard as he could. If he'd hit me with that, I'd have gone through the wall. But because my reach was five inches longer than his, his powerful punch just arced beneath my arm. He couldn't even touch me.

"If I was fighting a guy like you, Walt," he explained, "and you could hit anywhere near as hard as I could, you would *annihilate* me. I'd never get close enough to hit you. I learned that long ago, so I developed a style: cover-up, *peekaboo*. I took the blows on my arms, my shoulders, and sometimes on my face—five, six, seven, eight to one—because I knew if I could get in close enough, I could take them out with one shot." And he could. All he needed was the one shot.

Get in close with the Word of God, whatever it takes. . . . It's God's shot and God's gospel.

All of a sudden a light went on in my head, and I said, "Praise the Lord!"

"What are you praising the Lord for?" he asked.

"You gave me a fabulous sermon illustration. I'm going to make that illustration famous!"

"Well, what is it?"

"You accepted the occupational hazard of getting hit so that you might be a champion."

You and I have to accept the occupational difficulty and all of the occupational problems that come with the Christian witness. Get in close with the Word of God, whatever it takes. No matter how much punishment you have to endure or whatever they may say about you, get in close until you get the one clean shot that will take anybody out. It's God's shot and God's gospel.

—◦ ◦—

Something to Think About

How long has it been since *you* "got in close" with the Word of God?

A glorious band, the chosen few
On whom the Spirit came,
Twelve valiant saints, their hope they knew,
And mocked the cross and flame:
They met the tyrant's brandished steel,
The lion's gory mane;
They bowed their necks the death to feel:
Who follows in their train?
  —"The Son of God Goes Forth to War"

Something to Do

Pray first and ask the Holy Spirit to open your eyes to God's teaching. Read Luke 8:16–21. Ask God for the privilege of sharing your faith with someone today.

2

Who Is the Lord?

Pharaoh said, "Who is the Lord, that I should obey him and let Israel go? I do not know the Lord and I will not let Israel go."

—Exodus 5:2

Moses. Forty years living it up in Egypt, forty years repenting in Midian, and then forty years doing what he was supposed to do to begin with. Sound familiar? That's your life and mine, maybe not 120 years worth, but chop it up any way you like—that's the way the cookie crumbles. We've all been the Moses way: prince of Egypt, shepherd of Midian, prophet of the living God. The Lord called him at the age of eighty, "It's time to go, Moses, back into Egypt."

Moses said, *"I can't,* Lord. My picture's up in every post office. I'm wanted for murder! The KGB, the CIA, and everybody in Pharaoh's organization have got my name up there. The minute I show up, I've had it."

The Lord said, *"Go,* Moses. I will go with you. My presence will go before you."

The vastness of energy that cannot be calculated was placed at the disposal of an eighty-year-old man. God said, "What do you have to worry about? The force that holds the galaxies together will go before you. Just go."

Moses said, "Yes, Lord." And back he went.

We all know the story of how he had a little argument with Pharaoh, and Pharaoh, in one of the greatest dialogues of all history said, "Who is the Lord that I should listen to him?" I'm sure Moses looked him right in the eye and replied, *"You should live so long!* Who is the Lord? You should find out who the Lord is. Let my people go." Pharaoh wouldn't.

The Lord said, "It's all right. I know he won't let them go. When I get finished with him, believe me, he will *give* you the land of Egypt just to get rid of you. Who is the Lord? Wait and see."

"What do you have to worry about? The force that holds the galaxies together will go before you. Just go!"

Moses led them out of the land of Egypt. They got to the shores of the Red Sea, but the Egyptians changed their minds. Pharaoh said, "I must have been thinking *crazy* to let those Jews out of here. Go get them!" And he whipped into his chariot and took off with his crack troops.

There was Moses: Pharaoh chasing him with a vengeance, the sea in front of him, and the desert on either side. I don't think that's an enviable position militarily. Moses, whatever he was, was not General MacArthur. So Moses said, "I must talk with the Lord," and he went and prayed.

When he came out, he was radiant, and the people asked, "What are we going to do?"

Moses replied, "Don't worry. Get everybody ready and walk up to the edge of the water."

"What are we going to do? Boats?"

"No, we'll just walk over."

So, *two million people* start to walk toward the water, and this old man lifted his rod and the waters rolled back. Now you may say, "That's an incredible thing; the waters rolled back. I mean, you don't truly believe something like that do you?"

You better believe I do! The God that holds a billion galaxies together can open the waters of the Pacific Ocean like an envelope on a Monday morning! He's not going to have any problem with the Red Sea. It's a little drainage ditch in the Mediterranean. God just said, "Now!" and the waters rolled back.

Oh, the higher critics have had fun with this one. "A strong east wind blew over the Sea of Reeds, and it was very marshy, so the wind dried out the land. Then Moses and these marvelous, faithful Jews marched across that ankle deep water—two million of them—to the other side. That was the miracle."

The people who talk like this have lost their marbles! They've given us a greater miracle than we ever asked for, because if that's the case, *the Egyptians drowned a whole army in six inches of water!* That's a bigger miracle than opening the sea. God said, "Moses, lift up your staff, and I'll take care of the sea."

Who is the Lord? You should find out who the Lord is!

Something to Think About

God has something unique for you to do, because *you are unique.* Do you believe God is able?

> *Immortal, invisible*
> *God only wise,*
> *In light inaccessible*
> *hid from our eyes,*
> *Most blessed, most glorious,*
> *the Ancient of Days,*
> *Almighty, victorious,*
> *thy great name we praise.*
> —"Immortal, Invisible, God Only Wise"

Something to Do

Read Romans 8:28. Think of two things you love to do—then ask God to use these things for his glory. And when you pray, pray believing.

3

The Army of God

Finally, be strong in the Lord and in his mighty power. Put on the full armor of God so that you can take your stand against the devil's schemes. For our struggle is not against flesh and blood, but against the rulers, against the authorities, against the powers of this dark world and against the spiritual forces of evil in the heavenly realms.

—Ephesians 6:10–12

A spiritual war is going on, and it is directed against the Church. It is directed against all true Christian denominations, and against all true believers in them or outside of them. It is a premeditated, planned, open conspiracy to destroy, and it was launched by Lucifer, the prince of darkness, more than two thousand years ago.

The Scripture tells you right here that spiritual warfare is first, foremost, and primarily against the forces of darkness—against Satan and against satanic powers. But that's not all that's involved in spiritual warfare. We first have to recognize the *fact* of spiritual warfare. Some people act as if there were nothing going on around them—as if they were floating over Niagara Falls like a Ping-Pong ball, just bobbing along with nothing affecting them. When something adverse occurs in their lives, they never think of it as an attack of the devil. Instead, they just sort of say, "Well, that's life! That's the way things are," and they brush it off.

Not to worry—God will get your attention. There is such a thing as spiritual conflict. We are born into conflict: in conflict against the world, in conflict against our carnal natures, in conflict against the devil. We will live in that conflict and we will die in that conflict, unless Jesus Christ returns in our lifetime.

The Bible clearly tells us there is such a thing as spiritual war. It's our warfare; it's *personal* war. It's not against people. It's against the rulers of the darkness of this age that manipulate people as if this were a great chessboard on earth. And the forces are arrayed against the Christian church.

Now, of course, you have an option: you can be dumb. You can say, "I don't have any spiritual war, I think positively all the time. I don't have negative thoughts. I think only about possibilities and the things God has for me. There's no war around me." That's reminiscent of the Christian Scientist in hell who sat by himself in a corner and said, "I'm not here, I'm not here, I'm not here." But it never changes the fact—he's there! You are in a spiritual war whether you think so or not. The whole world is blowing up around you, and you just can't sit there and say, "Nothing's hap-pen-ing."

> *The Bible clearly tells us there is such a thing as spiritual war. It's our warfare; it's personal war.*

It is! And it will continue to happen, because the moment you enlist in the army of God you personally become a target. No more Mr. Nice Guy. You are on the satanic hit list. You are in the army of God.

If you will not fight in the army of God, then the Lord will discipline you until you get to the place where you will fight. You will get so many attacks that you will eventually have to do something. That is a warning. It is also biblical theology.

You are in the middle of a war. People who walk around in the middle of a war acting as if there is no war are called *casualties*. There are people scattered all over the landscape who are ineffective in their Christian lives, neutralized in their Christian witness, paralyzed in their Christian activities, simply because they don't realize they're casualties. They must be restored by God so they can get back into the battle.

―○ ○―

Something to Think About

God believes in *you*, and he wants you to believe in yourself. Don't be discouraged. You are in the middle of a war, but—take heart—you do not fight alone.

Like a mighty army
Moves the church of God;
Brothers, we are treading
Where the saints have trod;
We are not divided;
All one body we,
One in hope and doctrine,
One in charity.
Onward, Christian soldiers,
Marching as to war,
With the cross of Jesus
Going on before!
—"Onward, Christian Soldiers"

Something to Do

Read Matthew 10:29–31. Remember this: God surrendered his beloved son to a cruel death—to save *your* life. Kneel before him and rededicate your life to his service.

4

Don't Give Up

"For God so loved the world that he gave his one and only Son, that whoever believes in him shall not perish but have eternal life."

—John 3:16

I had a very good friend; we grew up together. He was really my brother's buddy, but I loved him just like an older brother. He was the most blasphemous, womanizing, boozing, absolutely degenerate human being I have ever met in my entire life—and I've met about every kind there is. He made his money in oil and he could buy anything he wanted, and he did. Every time I'd witness to him he would say, "You don't really believe this Jesus stuff, do you?" And with that he'd really *zing* me. I witnessed to him until I was purple in the face. Man, he roasted me every chance he got. You would say, "It's impossible! God's never going to do anything with that kind of man."

Well, I met him in Singapore a few years ago, and while we were chatting, I began telling him about the Lord. Oh, he wouldn't have anything to do with it. He didn't "need any of this stuff," and he went on and on about it. A few months later he came back to the United States. He had contracted a rare disease: an inflammation of the lining of the heart. And suddenly, this great brute of a man was reduced to a shadow of himself: All of his money couldn't help him, all his women were memories, and all his strength was gone. Everything he had ever leaned on all of his life had disintegrated and disappeared.

I made a special trip to the hospital to see him, and he was lying in bed, frail and hopelessly sick. When I came into the room he recognized me and said, "Help me up." So I gently pulled him up in the bed. He put his head down and whispered, "I'm dying."

"Did the doctor tell you that?" I asked.

"Yes."

"Are you sure you're going to die?"

"Yes," he answered. "Everything's in order." His lip trembled. He was a courageous man.

"It isn't," I said.

"What? What do you mean?"

> *"The Lord Jesus is here for you. . . . Why don't you trust Christ?"*

"It isn't in order, Jack. It's not in order with God. But I've got some wonderful news! What I've been telling you all these years is still true. The Lord Jesus is here for you and he wants to save you. Why don't you trust Christ?" And then I witnessed to him.

Afterward I took him by that great, massive paw of his and I asked, "Jackie, do you want Jesus?" The tears rolled down his hardened face and he responded, "Yes, I *need* him." And we prayed together. That night, in just a moment of time, Jesus Christ came into that room, and into that man's life, and into his soul—and he was born again. *Don't ever give up on people.*

Something to Think About

Do things seem hopeless to you? They're not! The Holy Spirit is working quietly, consistently, patiently—*powerfully*.

> *Softly and tenderly Jesus is calling,*
> *Calling for you and for me;*
> *See, on the portals he's waiting and watching,*
> *Watching for you and for me.*
>
> *Come home, come home,*
> *Ye who are weary, come home;*
> *Earnestly, tenderly, Jesus is calling—*
> *Calling, O sinner, come home!*
> —"Softly and Tenderly"

Something to Do

Study Luke 11:5–13. Be bold.

5

_꜀ꜞ ꜞ꜀_

Where Is Your Heart?

"Do not let your hearts be troubled. Trust in God; trust also in me. In my Father's house are many rooms; if it were not so, I would have told you. I am going there to prepare a place for you. And if I go and prepare a place for you, I will come back and take you to be with me that you also may be where I am."
—John 14:1–3

There was no room at the inn for Jesus, but there's room at the cross for you. There's room for people in the kingdom of God.

God says he's prepared a place for you. The picture is of a great oriental palace, very popular in those days. This palace has many, many rooms in it—luxurious suites, all the way down to closet-sized accommodations. You are going to inherit a room in the palace which is in direct proportion to your life of service for Christ. In other words, salvation is God's gift to everyone, but the blessings of heaven and eternity are individually bestowed on the basis of one's life of dedication and service for Christ.

That's why Jesus said, "Do not store up for yourselves treasures on earth," because the moth and the rust corrupt it, and the thieves break through and steal it (Matt. 6:19–21). But lay up for yourselves treasures in heaven, because if your reservation is there, *nobody cancels it.* If your reservation is there, the moth and the rust can't corrupt it, and the thieves can't even get near it.

So "where your treasure is, there your heart will be also." If you're looking forward to being in the presence of Christ and can't wait for the joy of seeing him, then your heart's there and your treasure's there. Unfortunately, too many people have one foot on earth and the other foot in heaven. God calls us to be living sacrifices. The problem with living sacrifices is they have a nasty habit of squirming off the altar. Far too many people are trying to feather their beds on earth when they should be storing up treasures in heaven.

How do you store treasures in heaven? You do it by prayer, supplication, and thanksgiving. You store treasures in heaven by service to God; by presenting your body as a living sacrifice, holy and acceptable to God. You lay up treasures in heaven when you permit the fruits of the Spirit to blossom in your life: "love, joy, peace, patience, kindness, goodness, faithfulness, gentleness and self-control" (Gal. 5:22–23). You're allowing treasures to be stored for you when you allow the Holy Spirit to live in you and work through you to touch the lives of others. Even a cup of water in the Master's name will not go without its reward (Mark 9:41).

Do you want to know how to store treasures in heaven? Obey God now.

Do you want to know how to store treasures in heaven? *Obey God now.* Let the fruits of the Spirit, the power of the Spirit, and the life of Christ be part of your life. You want to be sure of having great treasures in heaven? Then don't set any store on the permanency of your possessions on earth.

Let the life of Christ be lived in you. You can't do it yourself—let Christ do it. "I can do everything through him who gives me strength" (Phil. 4:13).

—◌ ◌—

Something to Think About

What's truly important to you? How would you spend the last few hours of your life?

> *Take my love, my God, I pour*
> *At Thy feet its treasure store;*
> *Take myself and I will be*
> *Ever, only, all for Thee,*
> *Ever, only, all for Thee.*
> —"Take My Life and Let It Be"

—⟨⟩ ⟨⟩—

Something to Do

Reserve some time for God today and reassess your priorities. Where is your treasure?

6

_〜 〰_

Silent Witness

"Blessed are you when men hate you, when they exclude you and insult you and reject your name as evil, because of the Son of Man. Rejoice in that day and leap for joy, because great is your reward in heaven."

—Luke 6:22–23

One of the main problems today, and one of the reasons we are in crises, is that a large segment of Christians will not come into conflict with the world. That is one of our greatest drawbacks. So many Christians are waiting for a *convenient* time that the gospel never gets preached. So many Christians say, as I've had people say to me on numerous occasions, "I don't talk about my faith, I live it. People can see my faith in what I do, but I never talk about it too much. I'm a silent witness."

You bet you are! You're so silent nobody knows you *are* a witness. I can introduce you to numerous Jehovah's Witnesses, Mormons, Christian Scientists, atheists, and skeptics who are just as much silent witnesses from the standpoint of ethics, morality, and living as a great many Christians—and they're *lost*.

The New Testament doesn't know anything about a *silent witness*. The word *witness* is derived from the concept of *martyr*. You wouldn't be a martyr if you kept your mouth closed. The Christian church is studded throughout history with martyrs who proclaimed the truth as it is in Christ.

Now, I recognize that I may irritate a few people by saying things as bluntly as this, but the ministry is not a place for a popularity contest. The ministry is a place to tell it like it is, because we are in mortal danger today—the danger of not *communicating* because we think that in one way or another people are not going to like us. Whoever told Christians the world was going to like us or the world was going to love us? We are so preoccupied with whether or not the Masons, the Elks, the Shriners, and everyone's Uncle Harry are going to look upon us askance if we take a firm stand for Jesus Christ, that we are soft-pedaling the gospel up and down this nation and all over the world.

> *Whoever told Christians the world was going to like us or the world was going to love us?*

Let me illustrate what I mean: There are people who will go out and talk about the love of Jesus. They will talk about the fact that he died on the cross for our sins, that he rose from the dead, and that he is the Savior of lost men. They'll talk about that, and about the love of Christ and the need to be reborn spiritually—all well and good. But they will never, *ever* tell people what it's going to cost them if they don't believe the gospel! That's the other side of the coin.

Now, if you simply go out and tell people about the love of Jesus, and how Jesus Christ died for our sins, and how he has given us the task of bringing the world to salvation, people will say, "What very devoted, dedicated, religious people they are." But if you go out and tell them that Jesus said, "I am the way and the truth and the life. No one comes to the Father except through me"(John 14:6); if you tell them that the same Jesus who kissed the babies said, "Depart from me, you who are cursed, into the eternal fire prepared for the devil and his angels" (Matt. 25:41); if you tell people what it's going to cost them to reject Jesus Christ, instantly you become an arrogant, ignorant, dangerous fundamentalist—and a fanatic. As long as we do not tell the whole story, the world will tolerate us. But if we tell the world the whole truth, the world will hate us as it hated him. He told them the truth.

Controversy is part and parcel of the Christian heritage. You cannot escape it if you really want to serve Jesus Christ. The only way you can avoid controversy as a Christian is never to say anything except that which people want to hear. No one wants to hear they're lost. No one wants to hear there is eternal judgment. No one wants to hear about meeting Christ as the Judge instead of the Savior; yet this is precisely what the Church is committed to preaching.

—❦ ❦—

Something to Think About

Are you only saying things people want to hear? It's not too late to speak out.

> *Who is on the Lord's side?*
> *Who will serve the King?*
> *Who will be His helpers,*
> *Other lives to bring?*
>
> *Who will leave the world's side?*
> *Who will face the foe?*
> *Who is on the Lord's side?*
> *Who for Him will go?*
>
> *By Thy call of mercy,*
> *By Thy grace divine,*
> *We are on the Lord's side—*
> *Savior, we are Thine!*
>   —"Who Is on the Lord's Side?"

—❦ ❦—

Something to Do

Ask the Holy Spirit for *power:* power to serve God—power to make a difference in someone's life.

7

_જ઼ જ઼_

Mad at God

*But God said to Jonah, "Do you have a right to be
angry about the vine?"*

"I do," he said. "I am angry enough to die."

*But the Lord said, "You have been concerned about
this vine, though you did not tend it or make it grow.
It sprang up overnight and died overnight. But
Nineveh has more than a hundred and twenty thousand people who cannot tell their right hand from
their left, and many cattle as well. Should I not be
concerned about that great city?"*

—Jonah 4:9–11

How do you deal with being mad at God? When he says he's your
rock and fortress, and the whole house burns down, clear to the
ground, what do you do?

Well, I'd take a good, long look at my life and find out if I was
playing with matches. That's the first thing I'd do. If that wasn't the
case, the second thing I would do is go to the Lord and say, "I know,
Lord, that it is you who works all things 'together for good to them
that love [you], to them who are the called according to [your] purpose' (Rom. 8:28 KJV). I love you, and I am called according to your
purposes. Therefore, whatever is taking place in my life right now you
will not allow to become so great that I can't handle it." God is faithful. He will not allow you to be tested beyond your power to resist
temptation (1 Cor. 10:13). You have not yet resisted to the point of

18

shedding blood as martyrs have done before. So no matter how bad it is, you're still here. And that's a plus, because you can continue rebuilding with God.

As far as being mad at God is concerned, it's totally fruitless. If you are offending God by your anger, you're being petulant. Jonah got mad at God—look at the end of the book—and God rebuked him. If you're angry with God, the best way to deal with it is to get down on your knees and confess the sin. Tell him you're sorry for being mad at him—even though you're mad at him still. Ask him to help you not to be angry, and to forgive and restore you—and he will. He's so gracious, kind, patient, and loving to a race of people who are determined to pursue their own goals.

If you're angry with God, the best way to deal with it is to get down on your knees and confess the sin.

―∽ ∾―

Something to Think About

God is faithful. He will not allow you to be tested beyond your power to resist (1 Cor. 10:13).

> *Teach me to feel that thou art always nigh;*
> *Teach me the struggles of the soul to bear,*
> *To check the rising doubt, the rebel sigh;*
> *Teach me the patience of unanswered prayer.*
> —"Spirit of God, Descend Upon My Heart"

―∽ ∾―

Something to Do

Take a few moments and think of the good things in your life. Thank God for his kindness, his generosity, and his love.

8

_꙯ ꙯_

My Son, the Professor

Be on your guard; stand firm in the faith; be men of
courage; be strong.

—1 Corinthians 16:13

I taught apologetics and comparative religions in the East some time
ago, and there was a late night radio program that aired in forty-three
states. This nation is loaded with insomniacs. I don't know if you
know that or not, but from 12:00 A.M. until 5:00 A.M., NBC has
between eleven million and thirteen million people who listen to
radio talk programs. This program was the biggest one in the country.

My mother was an insomniac. She was a young Christian who
had been saved in her sixties, and she used to stay awake and listen
to the radio. One night, as she listened to this program, they had
nothing but atheists, agnostics, skeptics, rabbis, and liberal clergy-
men on, and they spent all their time roasting Christianity. Well,
Mother was a young Christian filled with zeal, and after four hours of
listening to the gospel being roasted, she called me up—at five
o'clock in the morning!

"Walter," she demanded, "did you hear Long John Nebel tonight?"

"Who?" I asked.

"You know, the Long John program on the radio?"

"No, I didn't—and Mother—it's five o'clock in the morning!"

"I know that, Dear, but you should have heard this program." And
she proceeded to tell me about it.

So I listened and agreed, "It's terrible, Mother."

"Did you ever hear the program?" she asked.

"Yes."

"What do you think of it?"

"I think it's phony."

"It is!"

"Absolutely!" I answered. "They never have anyone on there who speaks for the gospel."

"Thank you, Dear," she said. "Good night!" *Boom.* She hung up.

I didn't know what was going to happen, but she stayed up from 5:00 A.M. until 9:00 A.M. when NBC opened. Then she called them on the telephone, gave them a sermon, and told them they were discriminating against Christianity!

Well, normally they wouldn't pay much attention to a little old lady living in Scarsdale, but she ended by saying, "And my son—*the Professor*—he says your program is phony, and he speaks to thousands of people every year."

"Oh, it is?" they said. "Well, hmmm, maybe we'd better get him—who is he? . . . Well, all right! We'll get in touch."

Soon after that, I received a telephone call from the head of the program.

"This is Mr. Nebel. You're Professor Martin?"

"Yes," I answered.

"I understand you think our program is phony."

"That's right!"

"What's phony about it?"

"You've never had anybody on that program who's ever said a word for Jesus Christ. You have a friendly bunch of people there. You're an atheist, and all your friends are agnostics, skeptics, or liberals. The gospel has as much chance of getting a fair shake from you as the Jews did from Adolph Eichman."

There was dead silence on the phone.

Put on the whole armor of God!

Finally he said, "Ah-h-h . . . what would you do if you got on the program? Do you believe in God?"

"Of course I do."

"Well, I know ministers that don't."

"No, you don't know ministers that don't; you know *phonies* that don't. I'm a minister of the gospel."

"Will you appear on our program?" he asked.

"Certainly," I said.

"Good. You're on tomorrow night." *Put on the whole armor of God!*

I wasn't quite prepared for this. But every time I think about it, I praise the Lord that he is so gracious to keep us strong when we ourselves would turn away from challenges.

Controversy is part and parcel of the Christian heritage. You cannot escape it if you really want to serve Jesus Christ.

—◌◌—

Something to Think About

If you could talk to millions of people, for just five minutes, what would you say?

> *Help me the slow of heart to move*
> *By some clear, winning word of love;*
> *Teach me the wayward feet to stay,*
> *And guide them in the homeward way.*
> —"O Master, Let Me Walk with Thee"

—◌◌—

Something to Do

Contemplate Psalm 138:3–7. Take hold of God's promise and stand firm.

9

Preaching Jesus

*Put on the full armor of God so that you can take
your stand against the devil's schemes.*
—Ephesians 6:11

I went into NBC the next evening. I'd been teaching apologetics and
reasons for faith for years, but I had no idea what I was up against. I
prayed hard before I left home that night. "Lord," I said, "before the
world began you knew what was going to happen at this moment.
Anoint me with the Holy Spirit. I *must* have the answers tonight. If
ever I needed them, it's tonight."

I arrived at the studio, and a very friendly group was there waiting
for me: an atheist, an agnostic, a skeptic, a Christian Scientist, and a
rabbi. We shook hands right before air time, and for the first ten or
fifteen minutes everyone was very pleasant.

Then the moderator said to me, "What is it you believe, Professor
Martin?"

I replied, "I believe in Jesus Christ, the Son of God, and the Savior
of the world."

"Oh," the rabbi questioned, "you certainly don't mean to imply
that if a person doesn't believe in Jesus, they're lost?"

"Precisely, Sir," I said.

"*What?*"

"That's correct."

"Well, we must discuss this," he stated. The discussion lasted *five
hours,* and I'll never forget it.

It's amazing how God provides allies in the strangest places. Here I was, preaching the gospel and answering questions with everyone on me like a pack of dogs. The computers were clocking thousands of telephone calls; the table was filled with telegrams ranging from "Who is this nut?" to "Thank God somebody said something. I've been listening for nine years, and this is the first breath of fresh air." This went on and on. It was a wild evening! And about halfway through the program, I knew I was communicating fairly well, but the rabbi was giving me a hard time. I couldn't understand why he was always there with the right answer just at the commercial cutoff. I was puzzling over it when the man in the control room caught my eye and waved to me. I smiled and waved right back. He started waving rather frantically and signaled for me to come over there. So, I approached the control room, and he quickly took me back behind the machinery. I didn't realize it then, but he didn't want anyone to see us talking!

"I believe in Jesus Christ, the Son of God, and the Savior of the world."

He put his hand on my shoulder and said, "Listen, Doc, I'm a Roman Catholic and we can afford to argue afterward, but we're both Christians and they're going to hang us separately if we don't hang together. I'm going to brief you on what's going on here, and then you go in there and *give it to 'em.*"

"Fine, Brother!" I agreed.

"They're waiting for the station breaks," he explained. "When they see the station breaks coming, they over-talk you so you miss your point. Do you see what's happening?"

Realization dawned. "So that's what's going on!"

"That's the way it's done. I'll tell you what you do: about thirty seconds before the next station break comes up, start talking. I'll turn your microphone *up*, and I'll turn theirs *down*."

"Praise the Lord!" I said.

He punched me in the shoulder and grinned, "Go get 'em!"

Back on the air, we were talking for a few minutes when the rabbi argued, very insistently, "You Christians can't even prove, outside of the Bible, that Jesus Christ ever existed. That's one of Christianity's great documentary weaknesses." Well, at that moment we were approaching a station break, and the Lord gave me some references.

I turned to him, "Do you accept the Talmud, Rabbi?"

"Of course."

"It's a divine commentary." I asked, "Nothing can be taken away and nothing can be added? It's historically accurate?"

"Yes." He was very emphatic about it. The second hand on the clock slowly moved toward twelve.

"Well then, perhaps you would undertake to explain to our large audience why the Talmud calls Jesus of Nazareth a bastard—if he was never born." The last words that went out over NBC before that station break were "Jesus of Nazareth a bastard—if he was never born."

We went off the air for a commercial.

I wish I had a Polaroid of that classic moment. The moderator cringed, the rabbi looked stunned, and everyone else buried their heads in their hands. I looked at the control booth window, and the guy was grinning from ear to ear and giving me the thumbs-up sign. We came through like gangbusters! The computers went wild. Jews were calling in from all over New York.

We went back on the air a few minutes later, and the first words I said were, "Now, in the Talmud, Rabbi, it says that Jesus is illegitimate. Would you care to explain that?" He started to equivocate, and the Lord opened the door—it was wide open.

I said, "You knew that text was in the Talmud before I quoted it, didn't you?"

He looked me right in the eye and answered, "Yes."

"You knew Jesus was a historical person by your own records."

"Yes."

"But you were willing to lie to this vast audience in order to embarrass Christianity, and that's the reason I'm on this program tonight. You're all dishonest because you never give anyone a chance to deal with these things. You're always cutting in and cutting people off."

The moderator looked right at me then and said, "So, go ahead." I went ahead for thirty-five minutes and preached Jesus Christ uninterrupted.

I had more free time on radio in forty-three states, for eleven years after that, than any minister in the United States. Why? Because I put on the armor of God—with all my inadequacies and weaknesses—and marched out to do battle against the forces which have thrown us into crises today.

We were born into crises. You and I are the children of those who were boiled in oil, thrown to the lions, and crucified upside down. "Put on the full armor of God so that you can take your stand against the devil's schemes" (Eph. 6:11). That's what God wants us to do today. The answer to Christianity in crises is to get dressed for the battle and stand. There is no higher motive than love for our fellowman. Jesus loved them enough to die for them. There should be no higher motive for us than to love *him* enough to proclaim his gospel. "Always be prepared to give an answer to everyone who asks you to give the reason for the hope that you have" (1 Pet. 3:15).

Something to Think About

Could *you* defend your faith against an atheist? An agnostic? A skeptic? Would you?

> Give of your best to the Master,
> Give of the strength of your youth;
> Throw your soul's fresh, glowing ardor
> Into the battle for truth.
> Jesus has set the example;
> Dauntless was He, young and brave;
> Give Him your loyal devotion,
> Give Him the best that you have.
> —"Give of Your Best to the Master"

Something to Do

Make sure you know what you believe and *why* you believe it!

10

Rock the Boat!

*Yet when I preach the gospel, I cannot boast, for I am
compelled to preach. Woe to me if I do not preach the
gospel!*

—1 Corinthians 9:16

We are suffering today from an endemic disease. This disease in the
Christian world is known by its Latin name, *Nonrockaboatus*. What it
really means is—whatever you do, no rocka de boat! The
Nonrockaboatus mentality must stop. We must deal with our brothers
and sisters who have been asleep so long they make Rip van Winkle
look like a kindergartner.

The Church has been asleep while the kingdom of the cults has
grown to more than thirty-four million people in the United States
and on our mission fields. They outwork us; they outgive us; they
outsacrifice us. The Watchtower produces more literature in six
months than all the presses in the denominations can do in a year!
The Mormons are pushing forward at a rate where, by the year
2000—if Christ tarries—they will have twenty million Mormons.
Their number doubles every ten years! We're going to have twenty
million Mormons and one hundred thousand Mormon missionaries.
The effort will be computerized with every bit of technology they can
get their hands on—and they've got the money to do it. You think it's
hard now? It's going to be incredible later on.

This is why we have to mobilize our resources and our technology. We can't afford the luxury of doing our own thing anymore.

Either we hang together and get the job done, or they're going to hang us separately—you better believe it!

We are at war, and if you consider yourself a soldier of the cross, you had better start being one. If you're a soldier, you don't get yourself encumbered with the things of earth; you want to please him who has called you to be a soldier.

You may say, "Well, you seem pretty upset about this, Dr. Martin."

> *Either we hang together and get the job done, or they're going to hang us separately—you better believe it!*

I am! The Nonrockaboatus mentality, the "stupid lawyer" mentality, and the "slimy businessman" mentality is selling out the defense of the gospel so that today people do not have reasons for their faith anymore. They use a host of salvation and sanctification texts. They talk about their experiences with the Lord Jesus and how wonderful it is for you to get saved. But when they're asked to answer a question—they can't.

That's our business, the business of giving people reasons for faith. Who cares what people think of us? The only thing that matters is what Jesus Christ thinks. If you please everyone else and you don't please him—let me tell you something—you're in trouble! The name of the game is Jesus, not the world in which we find ourselves. The world is passing away.

You and I are committed to the proclamation of the common salvation and the defense of the faith. We do not need Charles Russell, Mary Baker Eddy, Ron Hubbard, Joseph Smith, or Brigham Young. The faith was once and for all delivered to the saints, almost two thousand years ago. All we will ever need is that faith and Jesus Christ.

—⚬ ⚬—

Something to Think About

God requires commitment.

> *Strong to meet the foe, marching as we go,*
> *While our cause, we know, must prevail;*
> *Shield and banner bright gleaming in the light,*
> *Battling for the right we ne'er can fail.*
> *—"Sound the Battle Cry!"*

—⚬ ⚬—

Something to Do

Look up the word *commitment* in your dictionary. Pray about it. What does commitment mean to you?

11

_⊙ ⊙_

An Encounter with Christ

"I tell you the truth, whoever accepts anyone I send accepts me; and whoever accepts me accepts the one who sent me."

—John 13:20

While flying back home from a seminar one day, I found myself seated next to a lady who was dripping with diamonds. She wore expensive clothes, carried a Gucci handbag, and was obviously well able to afford all the things that go along with affluence in our society today. She told me she was traveling to Palm Springs for Christmas vacation. She was a very successful realtor, looking forward to a wonderful time. She wanted to get a little sun.

We chatted for a few moments, and the Lord laid it on my heart that she needed the S-o-n, not the s-u-n. So, I took the opportunity to lead her into a conversation about the Lord Jesus Christ. She was a lapsed Roman Catholic who knew the gospel, but certainly was not living a Christian life. She didn't seem responsive to the things of God: she wasn't into the Scriptures and she wasn't even into church, except periodically. We had an interesting conversation and after a while she turned to me and commented, "You know, I have a feeling that you didn't sit in this seat by accident. I've got this feeling that I should be listening to you."

"Good!" I said. "That's the feeling God wants you to have. Listen to me, because I am telling you what God wants you to know."

It was a fulfillment of this passage in John. This lady was receiving me, and, at the same moment, she became aware that she was also dealing with God, not just with me. I had a marvelous opportunity to present the gospel to her. When I finished she said, "Here's my card. Could you tell me what radio station you're on in Seattle? What time is it on? I'd love to listen. And would you send me some information so I could read a bit and learn more about the Bible?"

"I certainly could!" I replied. And we had a wonderful time talking together. The lady had received the gospel. She had received it from me, but in receiving me she received Christ. She was not believing in him unto salvation, necessarily, but receiving his Word—listening to what he said.

You see, if people will not listen to Christ, if they will not listen to the Spirit, they're never going to listen to you or me. You can be the greatest preacher in the world, the greatest teacher, and the most dazzling logician. You can shatter people's arguments. You can give them unanswerable biblical rhetoric. You can quote verses from now until purgatory freezes over. You can stun them with your knowledge of the Word of God—and that's all you'll do. You'll stun them, but they will not have received the message.

Every witness we have as believers is an encounter with Christ.

You and I are not in the business of impressing people with ourselves—with how much we know or our Christian testimony. We're in the business of communicating the meaning of that testimony to the lives of others. The only way we can do that is through the Holy Spirit. Every witness we have as believers is an encounter with Christ. As Luther so eloquently put it, you and I are his hands, his feet, his voice, his body, speaking to a dying world.

―☙ ❧―

Something to Think About

Do you believe in the supernatural power of God? Ask him to let you see it at work.

> *Let my hands perform His bidding,*
> *Let my feet run in His ways;*
> *Let my eyes see Jesus only,*
> *Let my lips speak forth His praise.*
> *—"All for Jesus"*

Something to Do

Study Acts 26:9–18. Ask the Holy Spirit to teach you something new.

12

Get in Shape!

Endure hardship with us like a good soldier of Christ Jesus.

—2 Timothy 2:3

If you are going to be a good soldier of Jesus Christ, you must get into the best possible spiritual condition. If you're going to be a soldier—get in shape! You can't go out and fight hand-to-hand combat when you're loaded with flab. If you're sitting on your surpluses, the enemy is going to have you for breakfast, lunch, and dinner.

You have to go out there and burn the suet off your carcass. You

If you're sitting on your surpluses, the enemy is going to have you for breakfast, lunch, and dinner.

have to get the muscles hard and the reflexes geared up. You have to be able to respond, because if you can't respond in physical combat, you die. It's as simple as that. You must respond in spiritual combat or you are spiritually wounded, and you lay around moaning and groaning about all that has happened to you.

"Be self-controlled and alert. Your enemy the devil prowls around like a roaring lion looking for someone to devour. Resist him, standing firm in the faith, because you know that your brothers throughout the world are undergoing the same kind of sufferings" (1 Pet. 5:8–9).

You must be sober and vigilant. The word *sober* means "alert." There's no such thing as a sleepy, successful soldier. If you're sleepy, you will not be successful. If you're sleepy on guard duty you won't have to worry about the enemy; your own side will shoot you! Sleepy soldiers who are not alert have one thing in common: they're dead. So God said, "Do you want to fight in spiritual warfare? Be alert!" Secondly, be vigilant because your adversary, the devil, is stalking about as a roaring lion seeking whom he may devour. Only one thing can turn that lion into a pussycat, and that is to resist him steadfast in the faith of Christ.

Many Christians today have not combated the enemy. They have not fought back as servants of God, and that is why they are weak and ineffective.

Something to Think About

It's hard sometimes to think of yourself as a soldier—but God says it's true. Are you sitting on your surpluses?

> *Soldiers of Christ, arise and put your armor on,*
> *Strong in the strength which God supplies*
> *Thru His eternal Son;*
> *Strong in the Lord of hosts*
> *And in His mighty power;*
> *Who in the strength of Jesus trusts*
> *Is more than conqueror.*
> —"Soldiers of Christ, Arise"

Something to Do

Join a Bible study group at church. There is power in knowledge and strength in fellowship.

13

Show Me Your Glory

Then Moses said, "Now show me your glory."
And the LORD said, "I will cause all my goodness to
pass in front of you, and I will proclaim my name, the
LORD, in your presence. I will have mercy on whom I
will have mercy, and I will have compassion on whom
I will have compassion. But," he said, "you cannot
see my face, for no one may see me and live."
—Exodus 33:18–20

In the Old Testament when God was taking the Jews through the wilderness after their escape from Egypt, Moses honored and praised God for all the miracles that were done. He gave God all the glory. Moses knew the Lord intimately: he knew him in the burning bush and he knew him by revelation. But still, he wanted even more intimacy.

As Moses talked with God, God told him that he was pleased with what Moses had been doing—he'd been doing God's will. Immediately, Moses *seized* this opportunity. It's very beautiful, almost like a child talking to a parent. Moses asked, if God is pleased with him to, "show me your glory." What did that mean in the relationship Moses had with God? Moses asked to look upon God. In other words he said, "I want to see you as you really are!"

Now, you'd think that a creature talking that way to the infinite Creator would be an affront, but instead God was *delighted* with the dialogue. He answered, "Right! Tomorrow, come on up to the mountain, and I will show you my glory! But . . . you can't look at me, because if you do, you are no more."

That always intrigued me. God said, "Come on up, but you don't know what you're asking for. You are asking for intimate comradery with deity. You are asking to look into the face of eternity. You are asking to behold all power, all knowledge, all wisdom. You are asking to look at the radiance of the glory of God's very nature!" And you just can't do that, because if he should ever let you see that in your present form, you would be no more. "For no one can behold me and live."

That's why in the New Testament, the revelation of God is so intimate for us. That's why Jesus said, "Don't you know me, Philip, even after I have been among you such a long time?

What Moses was denied, we have beheld—the glory of God in the face of Jesus Christ!

Anyone who has seen me has seen the Father" (John 14:9). In other words Jesus said, "You are seeing all that God can safely reveal to you now, in the person of the Son." The Lord Jesus Christ is the very intimate glory of God.

Hebrews 1:3 says, "The Son is the radiance of God's glory and the exact representation of his being, sustaining all things by his powerful word."

When we come to know the Lord Jesus as our Savior, we come to experience God in a more intimate way. Moses wanted a more intimate relationship. What Moses was denied, we have beheld—the glory of God in the face of Jesus Christ!

―◌◌―

Something to Think About

Moses seized the opportunity to know God more intimately. What will you do?

> *There is a place of comfort sweet,*
> *Near to the heart of God,*
> *A place where we our Savior meet,*
> *Near to the heart of God.*
>
> *O Jesus, blest Redeemer,*
> *Sent from the heart of God,*
> *Hold us who wait before thee*
> *Near to the heart of God.*
> —"Near to the Heart of God"

Something to Do

Pray and ask God for the opportunity to know him better. *Seize it.*

14

Shaking Kingdoms

"He who is not with me is against me, and he who
does not gather with me scatters."
> —Matthew 12:30

Some time ago, I was invited to appear on a national Christian television program. I go on this program about twice a year, because it takes six months for them to recover from my previous appearance. I arrived in the studio and they put out the red carpet, shook hands with me, and sent me to makeup. As I was sitting there enjoying my coffee and doughnuts, a smiling assistant producer showed up and chirped, "Now, we want you to feel perfectly free and at liberty, you know. Just get out there and do your thing."

"Thank you!" I said. "I'm planning on doing that." Then they handed me a sheet of paper that read, "Try to be positive in everything you say." Saint Norman was there also—Vincent Peale. The obvious attitude was: whatever you do, don't get anybody upset!

I continued reading and it said, "Do not make any remarks about Jehovah's Witnesses, Mormons, or Christian Scientists." Well, that was it. I wanted to leave because I was insulted. Can you imagine inviting a world authority on a subject—one who's spent thirty-four years getting a reputation in the field—to come there and talk about "Mary Had a Little Lamb"? The only reason they invited me to the program was because of who I was. That's it. And when I got there, they wouldn't let me talk!

So I prayed, "Lord, give me some tact—that's not my long suit—so I can get this message across," and I walked down onto the set. We sat down, and the moderator smiled at me, "How are you, Dr. Martin? So good to see you." (He was a show-business type, you know.) He shook my hand and asked, "What's going on in the kingdom of the cults?"

I stared at him for a split second before I let him have it! "I'm not so much interested in what's going on in the kingdom of the cults as I am in what's going on in the church of Jesus Christ. *There's evil right at the altar of God,* and we're not doing anything about it!"

"There is?"

"Yes! If I had a few minutes, I'd tell you."

"Go right ahead," he said. And that was his first mistake. His second was deciding not to *shoot me* and commit suicide two minutes later!

I began, "Well, I'll tell you what it is. Do you know there are people today on Christian television and radio programs screeching for freedom of religion on our airways in the United States? They want freedom. They're out there with petitions against Madalyn Murray O'Hair. They want to stop all these things from encroaching upon our religious freedom, but they will deny you your rights under the Constitution of the United States to speak on the airways owned by the American people. Do you know that?"

> *One fisherman, filled with the Holy Spirit, stepped out on the street without even a megaphone, and three thousand people trampled each other to get to Calvary.*

"No!" he gasped.

"Yes! They hand you pieces of paper that say, 'Don't mention Mormons, Jehovah's Witnesses, and Christian Scientists!'" I thought I was very tactful. He almost died. He nearly had a coronary right on the middle of the set.

"That's *awful,*" he finally managed.

"Yes," I said. "Give me thirty seconds and I'll tell you why."

"Go right ahead."

"It's the day of Pentecost and the disciples were in the upper room. The Holy Spirit came upon the Church. Power such as the world has never seen flowed to fishermen, tax collectors—and from there, to Jerusalem, Judea, Samaria, and to the uttermost parts of the earth—shaking kingdoms, creating civilizations. God honored his promise to Abraham 'in thee will I bless all the kingdoms of the earth' (Gen. 12:3). Power! Peter stood up and preached a sermon, and three thousand people got saved. One fisherman, filled with the Holy Spirit, stepped out on the street without even a megaphone, and three thousand people trampled each other to get to Calvary. That's power such as the world has never seen before.

"And then Peter gathered them all into the upper room, and he proclaimed, 'Now, we're going to carry this message to the ends of the earth: Jerusalem! Judea! Samaria! The world is going to know about Jesus Christ! However, when you run into the Pharisees, the Sadducees, the scribes, and the Herodeans, don't say *anything negative!*'"

The audience roared, and the moderator laughed, "I think you made your point."

―❦ ❧―

Something to Think About

How much do you value the opinions of others?

> Come, Holy Spirit, heav'nly Dove,
> With all thy quick'ning powers,
> Kindle a flame of sacred love
> In these cold hearts of ours.

> Dear Lord, and shall we ever live
> At this poor dying rate?
> Our love so faint, so cold to Thee,
> And Thine to us so great!
> ―"Come, Holy Spirit, Heavenly Dove"

―❦ ❧―

Something to Do

Check out the meaning of the word *compromise*. Does it describe your walk? Your witness? Your life?

15

_⌒∽ ∽⌒_

Cowards to Conquerors

*Mary stood outside the tomb crying. As she wept, she
bent over to look into the tomb and saw two angels in
white, seated where Jesus' body had been, one at the
head and the other at the foot.*

They asked her, "Woman, why are you crying?"

*"They have taken my Lord away," she said, "and I
don't know where they have put him." At this, she
turned around and saw Jesus standing there, but she
did not realize that it was Jesus.*

*"Woman," he said, "why are you crying? Who is it
you are looking for?"*

*Thinking he was the gardener, she said, "Sir, if you
have carried him away, tell me where you have put
him, and I will get him."*

Jesus said to her, "Mary."

*She turned toward him and cried out in Aramaic,
"Rabboni!" (which means Teacher).*

—John 20:11–16

Nothing can be proven outside the testimony of witnesses or your
own eyewitness experience. You and I were not there when Jesus
Christ came out of the tomb, but hundreds of people saw him alive
with infallible proof.

One of the greatest psychological proofs of the Resurrection is
this: The same people who ran like scared rabbits when they took

Jesus captive and brought him up for trial—these same people, three days later, took a 180-degree turn. They suddenly chose to risk exactly the same death their Master had experienced. Psychologically, that's incredible, unless something happened.

If you believe every effect has a cause, what was the *cause of the effect*—the change in those disciples? We're not talking theology now, just plain old horse sense. What could have changed them from cowards to conquerors? Only one thing accounts for it: They saw him alive! When they saw him alive after they knew he was dead, they knew he had been placed in the tomb, and they knew there was a watch on the tomb to prevent anyone from stealing the body—when they saw this, then they knew the gospel was 100 percent true, and they were willing to die for it. And they did.

You and I were not there when Jesus Christ came out of the tomb, but hundreds of people saw him alive with infallible proof.

You don't die for a crazy Jewish carpenter whose body was stuffed in some ignominious Palestinian graveyard; *you* wouldn't and I wouldn't, and those boys were smart Jewish boys and *they* weren't going to, either. Something changed them: the fact that Jesus presented himself to them. Eyewitness testimony. One of the greatest of them all was in John 20. Eyewitness testimony shook the foundations of all of their thinking. When Jesus appeared to them, and they touched his wounds, they knew immediately he had to be the Son of God—because he was alive with infallible proof.

What is infallible proof? Science says that if there is any such thing as infallible proof, it is the repetition of the same experiment. Jesus rose from the dead and Mary Magdalene encountered him—experiment one. The women encountered him—experiment two. The disciples encountered him—experiment three. The apostles encountered him—experiment four. Five hundred people saw him after the Resurrection—experiment five. Each one of these is the repetition of the same experiment. They all encountered the same phenomenon. What was it? He was alive! That's what changed the history of the world.

Something to Think About

What would you have said and done if you were Mary?

Look, ye saints! the sight is glorious:
See the Man of Sorrows now;
From the fight returned victorious,
Ev'ry knee to him shall bow:
Crown him, crown him.
Crowns become the Victor's brow.
—"Look, Ye Saints! The Sight Is Glorious"

Something to Do

Try writing a short poem or song of praise to God today.
Remember—praise is for the benefit of man.

16

Divine Wisdom

For the message of the cross is foolishness to those who are perishing, but to us who are being saved it is the power of God.

For the foolishness of God is wiser than man's wisdom, and the weakness of God is stronger than man's strength.

—1 Corinthians 1:18, 25

"The foolishness of God" is a phrase which ought to cause every person who reads the Bible to stop short. What did the apostle mean when he wrote this? I can understand how human beings can be foolish because I deal with them every day. I can understand how I can be foolish because I have a long, accurate memory of the number of foolish things I've done. I can understand how the United Nations can be foolish—all you have to do is go there to see how the nations of the world can be foolish. I can understand every degree of foolishness that I confront in life, but I cannot for the life of me conceive of how *God* can be foolish. But here it is in Scripture.

So, I began my quest by going through the Scriptures trying to find out exactly what was God's foolishness. The first man I found in the Bible who was the perfect example of foolishness was a man named Noah. I have a friend, Dr. John Montgomery, who climbed Mt. Ararat and then wrote a book, *The Search for Noah's Ark*. Up there at 14,800 feet they have found an absolutely enormous hunk of wood. It's approximately 450 feet long; it looks to be about fifty to

43

seventy-five feet thick and about fifty feet wide. The image they've been able to see through the ice is at least the biblical dimensions— *at least.* Nobody knows what it is, but it's sitting up there in frozen water, perfectly preserved.

There are stories of what has been found there. I heard a tape recording of an elderly man who climbed Mt. Ararat with his grandfather when he was a boy. Once there, he stood on the deck of an enormous boat—and he described a boat as they were built in ancient times. He said the deck was put together with what looked like very large pegs, and it was so big he couldn't walk the entire distance of it without getting tired.

In addition to this account, there are testimonies of archaeologists and other people who were there. They estimate that approximately fifty million tons of lumber rests up there. I have actually held a piece of it in my hand. That lumber is white oak impregnated with pitch, and the Scripture says that God commanded Noah to cover the ark with pitch, inside and out. Interestingly enough, no white oak grows within two hundred miles of Mt. Ararat, and even if it did, what would it be doing at 14,800 feet? Dr. Montgomery said it's either the ark or the largest Turkish outhouse in all history! I am not in a position to debate the findings with Dr. Montgomery, but there was a man named Noah of historical validity.

It doesn't make any difference what the world says about you! The only thing that makes any difference is what God says.

The Lord said to Noah, "Build a barge!" So Noah started to build. You can imagine the reaction of the local neighborhood:

"What are you doing, Noah?"

"Oh, we're building a barge."

"Really, why are you building a barge?"

"Well, I talked with the Lord recently—the Creator of the universe—and he told me there's going to be a lot of water around here."

"There is? We're in the middle of the desert; what are you building this thing for? It's like building a sailboat in your basement. How are you going to get it out?"

"Well, God told me to build it. I'm going to build it."

This continued for *years and years.* This crazy old man—hammering, banging, and sawing—putting this monstrosity together. The neighbors must have thought he was ready for Happydale. Everyone laughed at crazy old Noah until it started to rain—then no one laughed anymore. That was the end. God deluged the earth with water.

Noah built his ark. He built it in the face of every kind of argument. He built his barge in the face of every kind of criticism. Noah went to work and built the barge: 120 years worth of building. Then he got inside and everyone laughed *until* it started to rain . . . and Noah survived.

It doesn't make any difference what the world says about you! The only thing that makes any difference is what *God* says. Noah believed the foolishness of God, "Build a barge," when there was no water. What is utterly incredible and totally foolish to you and me is the essence of divine wisdom.

What is the foolishness of God? It is divine wisdom demanding faith.

_꒰ ꒱_

Something to Think About

How important is the world's opinion to you? Can you shut out its voice and hear only God?

> *His oath, his covenant, his blood*
> *Support me in the whelming flood;*
> *When all around my soul gives way,*
> *He then is all my hope and stay.*
>
> *On Christ, the solid Rock, I stand;*
> *All other ground is sinking sand,*
> *All other ground is sinking sand.*
> —"The Solid Rock"

_꒰ ꒱_

Something to Do

Read and commit to memory Jeremiah 9:23–24.

17

_cᴏ ᴏ_

Take a Stand!

Always be prepared to give an answer to everyone who
asks you to give the reason for the hope that you have.
—1 Peter 3:15

The work of Christian apologetics is not to apologize for Christianity, nor is it to attempt to destroy other people. We are summoned by God, not only to preach Jesus Christ as the Redeemer of mankind, but also to be prepared to give answers.

One of the reasons why the Christian church is weak and impotent today, one of the reasons why the kingdom of cults and the occult is growing, is because Christians think that all we have to do is tell people Jesus loves them, hand out a tract, do some normal personal work, and that's the end of our responsibility. This is not the truth, nor is it biblical.

We are told by the apostle Paul to be set for the defense of the gospel (Phil. 1:16). This means that the gospel must be defended by the church! Someone once told me, when I was discussing the subject, "Well, you know, the gospel is like a lion. All you have to do is turn it loose, and it will defend itself." People are always using these illustrations and forgetting that Scripture says, "Contend for the faith" (Jude 1:3).

> We've lapsed into the error of believing that somehow or other it is negative to defend the gospel.

Paul was absorbed with the idea of being a soldier of the cross, a follower of the Lamb. God requires that we become absorbed in

46

exactly the same way. We must sanctify the Lord God in our hearts and be ready *always* to give to every man an answer. If we do this, we'll get the same effects the apostles got; we'll see the same results the church fathers saw—the great apologists of the first five centuries. But we must do it. We can't pass the buck anywhere else. In the words of that immortal Baptist theologian, Harry Truman, "The buck stops here!" We must shoulder the responsibility and we must be bold.

Something to Think About

Controversy for the sake of the gospel is a divine command.

> *Stand up, stand up for Jesus,*
> *Stand in his strength alone;*
> *The arm of flesh will fail you,*
> *Ye dare not trust your own:*
> *Put on the gospel armor,*
> *Each piece put on with prayer;*
> *Where duty calls, or danger,*
> *Be never wanting there.*
>
> —"Stand Up, Stand Up, for Jesus"

Something to Do

The word *absorb* means to engulf, to captivate. You must become absorbed, engulfed, and captivated by Jesus Christ if you are to represent him.

18

_⊸ ⊶_

A New Testament Revelation

*The Spirit clearly says that in later times some will
abandon the faith and follow deceiving spirits and
things taught by demons.*

—1 Timothy 4:1

This verse should arrest the attention of every Christian who takes the
New Testament seriously, because with one stroke of his pen under
the inspiration of the Holy Spirit, the apostle informs us that the
teaching of the demons exists. There is something that originates
with Satan but represents itself as pure religion and as truth.

In the Book of the Acts, chapter 16, I want to show you how the
doctrine of the demons works and how detailed and thorough it is.
It is not a theologian's pipe dream. It is a New Testament revelation.
The pity is that it's not preached very often, primarily because it can
get quite sticky. But we ought to face it. Nothing is ever solved by running from it, only by facing it in the power of Christ's resurrection.

In Acts 16 the apostle Paul was carrying on a glorious ministry of
evangelism. As he was preaching and carrying on this wonderful ministry, it was inevitable that Satan would make his appearance, and he
did. Now what type of appearance did he make? "Once when we
were going to the place of prayer, we were met by a slave girl who had
a spirit by which she predicted the future. She earned a great deal of
money for her owners by fortune-telling" (Acts 16:16). "Fortune-
telling" in the Greek is literally "python." This whole idea goes back
to an ancient Greek cult. They were worshipers of a demon god called

Pithios, who appeared on Mt. Olympus in the form of a snake. This girl represented this divinity. Through her powers she brought much gain to the people who utilized her services. Now, if you notice very carefully here, she followed Paul and cried out, "These men are servants of the Most High God, who are telling you the way to be saved" (Acts 16:17).

Please note this first: Satan is very pious. Satan clothes all forms of devilry in the most pious terminology. He announces to the world that Paul serves the Most High God. They are "telling you the way to be saved"—in the Greek they are saying "a way" of salvation. The definite article *the* is not there. Satan doesn't recommend Jesus Christ's gospel. What he actually said was that these are servants of the Most High God and they are showing *a* way of salvation. He's doing the same thing today: Jesus is an *aspect* of the truth; he is a *fragment* of the life. But under no circumstances will Satan acknowledge Jesus is eternal God incarnate—the only way, the only truth, the only life. Never!

> Nothing is ever solved by running from it, only by facing it in the power of Christ's resurrection.

This young girl walking behind them was crying out, but she wasn't doing the talking; and when the spirit was cast out, her masters were not happy. The Holy Spirit is very bad for business among demons. You'll notice that he ruins business for them all the time. This is why occultism fears the presence of the Spirit. They don't fear other spirits, but they fear Christians who are filled with the Holy Spirit. They want no part of Spirit-filled Christians. Why? Because Christians have power from God to overcome them!

Christ as *a way*—that is the first plank in the platform of the doctrine of the demons. Jesus as a way, but not *the way*. The spiritists say he is the greatest medium. The Baha'i say he is one of nine great, world prophetic manifestations of deity. The Jehovah's Witnesses say he's a super-angel named Michael. The Mormons say he's one god in a pantheon of divinities. But the record of the Scripture is that he is indeed the Lord God Jehovah himself in human form—and this they cannot face. That is why when Paul turned around and said, "In the name of Jesus Christ I command you to come out of her!"—it came out, because no power is capable of resisting the Lord Jesus.

Christ as *a way*—that is the kingdom of the occult and of the cults. You will notice it when you run across it in the doctrine of the demons. So ask questions, probe. Some people will say you're being obnoxious. No. You're just concerned—and you should be. The world in which we live is disintegrating because people are *not* concerned. The Church must be concerned—desperately concerned.

⁓⁓

Something to Think About

Remember this: No power is capable of resisting the Lord Jesus Christ.

> *And tho this world, with devils filled,*
> *Should threaten to undo us,*
> *We will not fear, for God hath willed*
> *His truth to triumph thro' us.*
> *The Prince of Darkness grim,*
> *We tremble not for him;*
> *His rage we can endure,*
> *For lo, his doom is sure,*
> *One little word shall fell him.*
>   —"A Mighty Fortress Is Our God"

⁓⁓

Something to Do

The first plank in the doctrine of the demons is this: Jesus as *a way,* not *the way.* Write down the answers to these questions: Who do the spiritists say that Jesus is? The Baha'i? The Jehovah's Witnesses? The Mormons? The Scriptures?

19

Perspective

I know that after I leave, savage wolves will come in among you and will not spare the flock. Even from your own number men will arise and distort the truth in order to draw away disciples after them.

—Acts 20:29–30

The attack upon the Church is twofold. Those who attack from without are called wolves. Christ warned of them. They are not Christian and their intent is to destroy the flock. Scripture says to put on the whole armor of God and resist them. Then, there are those sheep who are divisive Christians *within* the body of Christ. They foment division and strife by writing their own private doctrines and teaching what the Church has *never taught,* leading people into terrible spiritual disasters.

Anyone who gets up and hawks healing, telling you it's God's will to heal you "no matter what" has forgotten all systematic theology and has no education of biblical theology. God is the Sovereign of this universe, and you will not *compel* him to do anything, no matter what kind of faith you've got. He will be God!

The apostle Paul wrote that God wants to heal us. The Scripture says that God loves us. He wants to provide every good thing for us, but we are not living in an Edenic paradise. We are living in a cursed world. You are living in a body that is dying—right now. If you don't believe me, look in the mirror in the morning before you wash your face. You think you'll never get lines under your eyes and sagging under your chin, and that your hair will never change color or disappear? You're a dreamer. You can exercise all the faith you want, but you'll still wear eyeglasses. You can exercise

Do not fall victim to the idea that your faith can dictate the will of God, because it can't.

all the faith you want, but you'll have china choppers for your teeth. You can talk about faith, faith, faith from now until the second coming of Jesus Christ, but if the sovereign God of the universe does not want to heal you, *he will not do it*. It's as simple as that.

Now, we should proclaim divine healing. We should proclaim salvation. We should proclaim all the benefits that come through the atonement of Jesus Christ. But, brothers and sisters, do not fall victim to the idea that your faith can dictate the will of God, because it can't.

There are some people God wants sick. Now you say, "How do you know that?" Because he said so! Exodus 4:11 says, "Who gave man his mouth? Who makes him deaf or dumb? Who gives him sight or makes him blind? Is it not I, the Lord?" What do you think he meant? You don't have to be a biblical scholar to figure that out. He said, "For my own sovereign purposes I allow these things to happen."

It is not wrong to urge people to faith. It is not wrong to rely upon the Word of God for the salvation of the soul, and for the healing of the mind and the body. This is, of course, biblical theology. But when it gets so far out of perspective that there are whole movements within the Church, and the lives of people are disrupted and confusion begins to reign—then it is necessary for the historic view of the Christian church to come out in the open for everyone to hear.

Something to Think About

God wants to provide every good thing for us, but we are not living in an Edenic paradise. We are living in a cursed world.

> *Be still, my soul—the Lord is on thy side!*
> *Bear patiently the cross of grief or pain;*
> *Leave to thy God to order and provide—*
> *In every change He faithful will remain.*
> *Be still, my soul—thy best, thy heavenly Friend*
> *Thru thorny ways leads to a joyful end.*
>
> —"Be Still, My Soul"

Something to Do

Study John 9:1-3. Why was this man born blind?

20

No Compromise

But Daniel resolved not to defile himself with the royal food and wine, and he asked the chief official for permission not to defile himself this way.
— Daniel 1:8

This passage has something very unique for us as believers to appropriate in our lives. Here is the context: a powerful king's world government and a group of young Jews taken into it and given every opportunity. They had wisdom, stature, poise, and learning. They were going to be trained for three years in "graduate studies" in the Babylonian language and culture. In other words, they were getting the Stanford University of their day.

To encourage them and give them stature in the community, the king's own table was made available to them. Now, you must understand exactly what that means. When King Nebuchadnezzar, the world's greatest reigning monarch at the time, invited you to his dining table, it meant honor, position, and recognition throughout his entire kingdom. He was a very great king, mentioned many times in the Scripture. These young men were given everything they wanted: privilege, class, power.

How might Daniel have reacted? "Golly gee, I've got this great opportunity! I've been selected over hundreds of thousands of potential students. Here I am, given a chance to eat the king's food, drink the king's wine, and live in the king's palace. My social security payments are now up-to-date. I have nothing but a good future ahead of me." In the ancient world, Daniel had it made. The world was his oyster. Is this what he thought? Was he a company man? Did he want to go along and get along with everyone and everything, as the world today would see it? That's the way people are. You have to go along and get along, right?

No! Daniel had different ideas. He thought, *I am selected by God. I'm one of God's children. I'm supposed to live as God wants me to live. Does God want me to sit at the table of a pagan king and eat food sacrificed to demons? No. Does God want me to defile myself for any purpose whatsoever? No.*

Can you hear the people of the time giving Daniel advice—some of the Jews, perhaps? "Daniel, you've never had it so good. Think how powerful you can be in the palace. Think of the authority you can wield to help your people. Whatever you do,

> *If we are seeking power from God, then we have to meet God on God's terms.*

be sure you get this kind of power because it will protect us." Now, that's good political advice. But Daniel turned 180 degrees away from that and decided, "I can't do this. I belong to God. I've got to do that which will glorify God. I will not defile myself."

You see, Daniel saw it in its proper perspective: What looked like good politics, what looked like common sense, what looked like conventional wisdom—was a trap. It would really defile.

That's something we have to learn. There are all kinds of opportunities offered to us. The kingdoms of this world proffer many things to the Church and to Christians. Today, all kinds of philosophies just like this are running loose all around us. We have to see them for what they really are: a means of entrapping us to make us "company" men and women; to get us to *get along by going along.*

Now, am I saying you shouldn't grab opportunities or that you shouldn't advance? No, of course not. We should all advance as God gives us the opportunity. But what price do you pay for advancement? If you pay the price of defilement; if you pay the price of compromise; if you pay the price of giving in on your principles and what you know God wants from you in your life—the price is too great.

Daniel wanted power from God, just as we want power in our lives. But if we are seeking power from God, then we have to meet God on God's terms, because the power originates with him. We're not going to receive it in our lives unless we meet him on that ground. Daniel is a noncompromising believer, a believer who takes personal purity and holiness to heart.

—⟶ ⟵—

Something to Think About

God wants to give you power. What does it mean to meet God on his terms?

> *Take time to be holy,*
> *Speak oft with thy Lord;*
> *Abide in Him always,*
> *And feed on His Word:*
> *Make friends of God's children;*
> *Help those who are weak;*
> *Forgetting in nothing*
> *His blessing to seek.*
> —"Take Time to Be Holy"

—⟶ ⟵—

Something to Do

Read 1 Corinthians 12:1–11. Ask God to reveal the power of the Holy Spirit to you.

21

What Is Love?

While Paul was waiting for them in Athens, he was greatly distressed to see that the city was full of idols. So he reasoned in the synagogue with the Jews and the God-fearing Greeks, as well as in the marketplace day by day with those who happened to be there.

—Acts 17:16–17

When we see idolatry, we are supposed to be provoked. When we see evil, we are supposed to get exercised about it. If you can calmly walk

> *The Holy Spirit is provoked by evil, and he stirs up the Church so that we may do something about it.*

through this upholstered cesspool of earth; if you can see evil, filth, degeneracy, and hear vile language; if you can see the corruption of the media and the perversion of the gospel; if you can see the multiple forms of idolatry—the worship of things and of the creation more than the Creator; if you can see this today and you are *not* provoked about it, then you are not in touch with God the Holy Spirit. The Holy Spirit is provoked by evil, and he stirs up the Church so that we may do something about it.

Christianity is not passive. Christianity is vigorously active! Paul, a Hebrew of the Hebrews, blameless, trained under Gamaliel with his Ph.D. at the University of Damascus, stood in Athens. He looked around, saw idolatry, and got angry in his spiritual nature. Notice, the Scripture says *he did something about it.* He went out to try and reason with them.

Do you know what happens to people today when the Holy Spirit stirs them up? They turn on their television sets and skip prayer meeting. Am I right? I'm afraid that too often, it's true. But if you really are in the will of God, do you know what happens to you when the Holy Spirit provokes you? You go out and you *do something* about it. Paul went out and he argued.

Oh, we have people today who say, "Christians aren't supposed to argue. We're supposed to *love*." Gush, gush, gush. Let me ask you something. Do you think that argument for the truth *excludes* love? Love became flesh in Jesus Christ, and when love ran into the Pharisees, the Sadducees, the Herodeans, and the scribes, love *argued* with them!

Incarnate love has to tell the truth. If someone is dying, do you go to their hospital bed and "love" them so much you never tell them they're going to die in their sins? They are forever lost if you don't. What is love? Love is telling the truth!

Paul did not pick arguments. He went out and he witnessed for Jesus Christ, and when people argued with him, he answered them. Christians are supposed to give answers to the world. We are not supposed to go about looking for arguments, but we must love people so much that we are willing to argue for the truth.

_ᴄ⊃ ᴄ⊋_

Something to Think About

Christianity is not passive. Christianity is vigorously active!

> *I am resolved no longer to linger,*
> *Charmed by the world's delight;*
> *Things that are higher,*
> *Things that are nobler,*
> *These have allured my sight.*
>
> *I am resolved, and who will go with me?*
> *Come, friends, without delay,*
> *Taught by the Bible, led by the Spirit,*
> *We'll walk the heavenly way.*
> —"I Am Resolved"

_ᴄ⊃ ᴄ⊋_

Something to Do

The next time you're provoked by evil, *do something about it.* Make a phone call, write a letter, tell a friend. Pray.

22

Incarnate Love

*Am I now trying to win the approval of men, or of
God? Or am I trying to please men? If I were still try-
ing to please men, I would not be a servant of Christ.*
— Galatians 1:10

I was a guest on another television program one evening. I get on this
one about twice a year. The hosts, a man and a woman who will
remain nameless, were asking me questions, and the lady got a little
upset with me. She said, "Dr. Martin, no one can gainsay the work
you've done in the world of the cults. We just praise and thank the
Lord for that."

Whenever I hear something like that, I know what's coming next:
I'm going to get shot!

"However," she continued, "I do have a constructive criticism to
make."

"What is it?" I asked.

"You don't show enough love. You've really got to love these people."

This was unbelievable! "I have been thirty-four years doing your
job and you're telling me I don't love them? What have you done?"

"I, ah, um. I don't want to get into a controversy."

"You're in one, Lady! This is my ballpark and my game, played by
my rules—and here it is straight out: I love Mormons; I love Jehovah's
Witnesses; I love the people in the cults. I gave my life, I'm giving my

life now, and I'll give it until the day I go home to glory, and cultism goes to its home in hell.

"I love them. I care. I'm fighting for their lives, for their souls. That's love! Love isn't this sickly, gooey, syrupy garbage that flows out, where people are forever saying with this plastic evangelical smile plastered to their faces, 'Jesus loves you. Jesus loves you. We want you to be born again.' Butter wouldn't melt in their mouths! In the name of God, people are dying in their sins. You have to tell them more than 'Jesus loves you.' You have to tell them Jesus is going to judge them! If they're not going to receive love, they're going to receive justice.

> *"I love people. I care. I'm fighting for their lives, for their souls."*

"An old Nazarene preacher said something to me at the beginning of my ministry that I never forgot. He said, 'Walt, I love to hear you preach because you crack all the nuts everyone runs away from. Don't ever give up doing it. Just go out there and do it, and remember something, Son: When you get out there give 'em Jesus and the gospel of grace and love—but if they're not going to buy it, be sure you leave 'em with Moses.'"

There was utter silence in the studio. After a moment I said, "I never forgot that advice. He was telling the truth. You don't want grace? OK, let me introduce you to some law. If you're not going to be saved by grace, you'll be judged by God's Law. The one thing I don't want when I stand in the presence of God is to be judged on the basis of law. I want mercy—I don't know about you—all I can get!"

Well, the lady seemed a little stunned, but after a moment she said, "Uh, I don't want to get into a discussion. . . ."

"Look, give me thirty seconds, and I'll prove it to you."

"Oh, go ahead," she snapped.

I said, "I want you to listen to the voice of incarnate love. Who was the most loving person who ever lived?"

"Why, Jesus!"

"That's right. Jesus was incarnate love, wasn't he? Love in human flesh, right?"

"Right."

"Good. Listen to him. 'You generation of slimy snakes, who warned you to flee from the damnation of hell? You whitewashed sepulchers on the inside filled with rotting corpses . . . you children of the devil. The lusts of your father you will do. He was a liar and a murderer from the beginning and he abode not in the truth. I am from above. You are from beneath. You will seek me but you will not find me. You will die in your sins for where I am going you cannot come." (Matt. 23:27, 33; John 8:23, 44)

Once again, there was dead silence in the studio. And then this lady said to me—I kid you not—"Couldn't you smile a little bit?"

Something to Think About

Do you love people? Do you care? Are you fighting for their lives, for their souls?

> O for a faith that will not shrink,
> Tho pressed by ev'ry foe,
> That will not tremble on the brink
> Of any earthly woe!
>
> A faith that shines more bright and clear
> When tempests rage without;
> That when in danger knows no fear,
> In darkness feels no doubt.
> —"O for a Faith That Will Not Shrink"

Something to Do

Find the word *love* in a concordance. How does Jesus define love in his teachings and demonstrate it in his daily life? Why is it so important to talk about judgment?

23

Smart Investing

"Then the King will say to those on his right, 'Come, you who are blessed by my Father; take your inheritance, the kingdom prepared for you since the creation of the world. For I was hungry and you gave me something to eat, I was thirsty and you gave me something to drink, I was a stranger and you invited me in, I needed clothes and you clothed me, I was sick and you looked after me, I was in prison and you came to visit me.'

"Then the righteous will answer him, 'Lord, when did we see you hungry and feed you, or thirsty and give you something to drink? When did we see you a stranger and invite you in, or needing clothes and clothe you? When did we see you sick or in prison and go to visit you?'

"The King will reply, 'I tell you the truth, whatever you did for one of the least of these brothers of mine, you did for me.'"

—Matthew 25:34–40

God gave mankind the capacity to do all of the above things, but the good and faithful servant is the one who invests the talents that God has given and does indeed become a servant to mankind. If the parable of the Good Samaritan means anything, it means that my neighbor is the person who needs me. The command is this: I should love my neighbor as I love myself.

It's obvious that if we, as professing believers, claim to have a relationship to Christ, then we must invest the talents of God. Jesus is not talking about investing money in this passage; he's talking about investing life. We are good and faithful servants to the degree that we invest our lives, our fortunes, our abilities, and the talents God has given us in service to our fellowman.

But the person who says, "I believe it," or the person who says, "I should do it," and *doesn't* do it, is the unfaithful servant. He is the one who has all the appearance of godliness but *disproves* the reality of Christianity in his life, because he does not love his neighbor as himself. If we can see our neighbors—the disenfranchised and the poor—and it never touches us; if we are not going to share our substance with those who are in need, how then do we fulfill this parable?

> *We are good and faithful servants to the degree that we invest our lives, our fortunes, our abilities, and the talents God has given us in service to our fellowman.*

The unprofitable servant is the one who, when people are hungry, doesn't feed them; when people are thirsty, doesn't give them drink. Jesus said, "Don't you recognize that I'm giving you all of these opportunities to show your devotion to me? Don't you realize that in caring for the least of these—with whom I identify—you are ministering to me?"

We are supposed to invest the talents that God has given us. If we shut our minds and spirits to the needs of others, how then are we profitable servants? One thing is absolutely certain in this parable: God is telling you—if you really are his child—that you had better invest what he has made available to you: time, substance, money, concern, and compassion.

—◌ ◌—

Something to Think About

Jesus said, "Don't you see? I'm giving you all of these opportunities to show your devotion to me."

> *O to be like Thee! Full of compassion,*
> *Loving, forgiving, tender and kind;*
> *Helping the helpless, cheering the fainting,*
> *Seeking the wandering sinner to find!*

O to be like Thee! O to be like Thee,
Blessed Redeemer, pure as Thou art!
Come in Thy sweetness, come in Thy fullness;
Stamp Thine own image deep on my heart.
                    —"O to Be Like Thee"

Something to Do

Write down one talent you know God has given you. *Invest it.*

24

_꧁ ꧂_

The Things God Cannot Do

> *And we know that in all things God works for the*
> *good of those who love him, who have been called*
> *according to his purpose.*
>
> —Romans 8:28

If God is good and if God is just, how in the world do we explain the existence of evil? How do we explain the problem of pain and suffering? How do we come to grips with a world which quite obviously is dominated not by good, but by forces which are quite the opposite? I think the Christian has to wake up to the fact that this kind of problem can't be swept under the rug.

First of all, the term *omnipotence* has to be defined as quickly as possible. What do we mean when we talk about omnipotence? Well, in the Latin from which it comes, it simply means "all powerful." So when we say that God has, as one of his primary attributes, omnipotence, we are talking about all power being vested in God. It is extremely important at this juncture that you understand this: All power does not mean the capacity to do anything the person who possesses it chooses! Omnipotence means "all power" but not necessarily the capacity to do anything that you wish to do.

So let's face it for what it is: There are things that God, though omnipotent, *cannot do.* These are the things contrary to his revealed nature. The Scripture says it is impossible for God to lie (Heb. 6:18). It is impossible for God to do something in eternity and then contradict it in time. It is impossible for God to fail. God cannot countenance sin;

64

he *cannot*, because he is Holy. There are at least fourteen or fifteen things the Scripture tells us God cannot—not "will not"—but *cannot* do. Limitations are imposed by God's character, by his nature. So as we face the problem of evil, let's understand the definition of omnipotence.

If a beneficent, omnipotent God exists, he could annihilate evil at will, and he could end all pain and suffering anytime he chooses. A being who has the power to do this would be cruel and unjust not to exercise it and thus end all evil and its consequences, right?

Here is the rub: If you are going to end all evil you must begin with evil *wherever* it may be. If God does this—then all of us are no longer here. All beings who have the power to choose have, within one thousandth of a second of his decree, ceased to exist. If the only way to deal with evil is to annihilate it as an actual and a potential, then you destroy its actual manifestation and you destroy its potential manifestation. And the moment you do that, you have successfully annihilated the entire human race.

> *If we're going to deal with the problem of evil, let's deal with it from the perspective of God, not from the perspective of men.*

Do you see what you're really trying to do? In effect, you're saying to God, "If I had the power, I could do it better than you can do it." But if we're given the power, hypothetically, we just *can't* do it.

If we're going to deal with the problem of evil, let's deal with it from the perspective of God, not from the perspective of men. The solution to evil is not instantaneous annihilation. The solution from God's perspective is: to work it all out for his glory and for man's redemption. It is no accident that Romans 8:28 remains one of the front pieces of divine revelation. Scripture tells us that God looks down on the evil that has come from free choice, and he says, "I will not intervene in it except to exercise *my free choice*, to cause the goals of evil to be turned to the ultimate glory of my purpose." God is not cruel and unjust. He is infinitely loving and patient, constantly and consistently working all things out for good.

―∽ ∾―

Something to Think About

Instead of annihilating us, God chose to transform us.

> *He breaks the power of canceled sin,*
> *He sets the prisoner free;*

His blood can make the foulest clean,
His blood availed for me.

Jesus, the name that calms my fears,
That bids my sorrows cease;
'Tis music in the sinner's ears;
'Tis life and health and peace.
    —"O for a Thousand Tongues to Sing"

Something to Do

Consider Philippians 3:20–21. Praise God for his great mercy and love.

25

Our Heritage

I have become its servant by the commission God gave me to present to you the word of God in its fullness—the mystery that has been kept hidden for ages and generations, but is now disclosed to the saints. To them God has chosen to make known among the Gentiles the glorious riches of this mystery, which is Christ in you, the hope of glory.

— Colossians 1:25–27

A few years ago I spoke with a friend of mine, the great basso profundo of the Metropolitan Opera, Jerome Hines. Jerry Hines is an exceptional Christian, a very gifted vocalist, and a brilliant man who holds a degree in physics.

Jerry went to Moscow during the time when Nikita Khrushchev was premier, and while there, he sang the great Russian opera *Boris Gudonov*. When he finished singing, Nikita Khrushchev jumped to his feet in the box where he was sitting and shouted at the top of his lungs, "Bravo! Bravo! Bravo!" He started to applaud, and the whole audience immediately jumped to its feet and shouted its approval.

Afterward, Khrushchev threw his arms around Jerry Hines, who is six feet six inches tall, and he said, "Gudonov! Gudonov!" For a moment, Jerry didn't know what he meant.

"Until you sang," Khrushchev explained, "I did not meet Boris Gudonov. When you sang, *you* were Gudonov! You were Russian. You are welcome in this country always to sing for us." It was an amazing thing.

Well, Jerry told me a story *behind* this story. There was a girl who sang opposite him, in the role of Boris Gudonov's son. The part is played by a female because it's a soprano role. Well, this girl was a devout Jehovah's Witness, and Jerry had spent a great deal of time trying to get her to come to Christ. He told me, "I tried everything I possibly could, Walter, and I couldn't get *any-where*. She was as hard as a block of granite. But when we were singing on that stage, a thought came to me. At that moment, I prayed as I do every time I go on stage, 'Please bless me tonight. Let me sing my best.' And then for some strange reason, I added, 'Lord, I pray for this girl that she might be born again. Lord, let her see Christ in me tonight. Be present on the stage with me. Let her see you instead of me.'"

> *"I looked into your eyes and saw your face, but it wasn't you."*

There is a great scene in this opera where Boris dies, and he sings to his son, "I'm dying, I'm dying." It's a very sad aria. Well, Jerry sang this lying on the bed with the girl sitting next to him looking into his face, and suddenly, when he got to this portion of the aria, the girl stopped acting. She just froze on stage, and then she started to weep. Tears coursed down her face and her whole body convulsed. Puzzled, Jerry grabbed her and kept on singing as she wept against his shoulder. Finally, he was able to whisper, "Are you all right?" She said, "Just a minute. Just a minute."

Later, when they came off the stage, Jerry said she shook all over, as if she were terrified. So he asked, "What's the matter? What happened to you?"

And she answered, "Something happened tonight during that aria. You must have felt it. I saw it!"

"What did you see?" he asked.

"It wasn't *you*. I looked into your eyes and saw your face, but it wasn't you. I wasn't even hearing your voice. It was another voice completely. *What is this?*"

At that moment Jerry knew what had happened: God had answered his prayer. "I have something wonderful to tell you," he said. "I prayed before I went on stage that you would see the Lord Jesus Christ dying for your sins—that you would see Jesus on the cross."

And at that, she just dissolved into tears on his shoulder.

You may say, "That's a mystical experience. That's a metaphysical experience. That's something beyond this earth!" Yes! Yes! Yes! But it happened on this earth for the glory of God. What did that girl see? She saw the holiness, the mystery of godlikeness in one brief moment in his face, and it destroyed all of her theological arguments, and all of her stoniness disappeared. He was able to witness to her then as he'd never done before.

That's our heritage: "Christ in you, the hope of glory." Pray that the mystery of godlikeness may be in our lives, that people may *see* we are set apart and sanctified for service to Jesus Christ. It is he who loved us, who died for our sins on the cross, and who rose from the dead. Because he lives, we live also.

With this knowledge, "Fight the good fight of the faith" (1 Tim. 6:12). Christ's righteousness, his mercy, his grace, and his godliness are our inheritance by faith.

_⟋⟍ ⟋⟍_

Something to Think About

"Christ in you, the hope of glory." This is your heritage.

> *Jesus is standing on trial still—*
> *You can be false to Him if you will,*
> *You can be faithful thru good or ill.*
> *What will you do with Jesus?*
>
> *What will you do with Jesus?*
> *Neutral you cannot be;*
> *Some day your heart will be asking,*
> *What will He do with me?*
> —"What Will You Do with Jesus?"

_⟋⟍ ⟋⟍_

Something to Do

Pray that the "mystery of godlikeness" may be in your life today—that people may see you are set apart.

26

Let God Deal with It

*Then the Lord rained down burning sulfur on Sodom
and Gomorrah—from the Lord out of the heavens.
Thus he overthrew those cities and the entire plain,
including all those living in the cities—and also the
vegetation in the land. But Lot's wife looked back and
she became a pillar of salt.*

—Genesis 19:24–26

What does this passage mean? God said, "When you leave Sodom—
do not look back!" Pretty simple?

Imagine yourself in Sodom and the angel of the Lord tells you,
"The Lord is going to destroy this city. It will
be a holocaust. It will go down in history.
They'll never be anything like this again.
Sodom and Gomorrah—gone forever off the
face of the earth. Now, get everything together
and get out of here! Once you go through the
gates of the city, *do not look back.* That's a divine command."

*Just keep going and
let God take care of
it.*

Everyone obeyed but Lot's wife. When the holocaust descended,
fire and sulphur from Jehovah out of heaven, she just couldn't resist
seeing those Sodomites get what was coming to them. So she turned
around—and got what was coming to her! She turned into a pillar of
salt because she disobeyed the Word of the Lord.

She wanted to *see* divine judgment. That's a warning to people
who want to see God balance the scales with other people. Leave

them alone. Walk away from it. Let God deal with the people. He'll take care of them. Don't you look back and say, "Oh, I can't wait to see what God's going to do to this person." Forget it. Remember Lot's wife. Just keep going and let God take care of it.

Something to Think About

How many times have you looked back?

I have long withstood His grace;
Long provoked Him to His face;
Would not hear His gracious calls,
Grieved Him by a thousand falls.

There for me my Savior stands,
Holding forth His wounded hands;
God is love! I know, I feel,
Jesus weeps and loves me still.
                    —"Depth of Mercy"

Something to Do

Let God deal with people. Read and commit to memory 1 Kings 8:38–39.

27

Fighting about Nothing

Don't grumble against each other, brothers, or you will be judged. The Judge is standing at the door!
—James 5:9

A great evangelist of the past once said that churches by and large have become places where we have soft lights, soft music, and even softer sermons—and as a result people have been lulled into a false sense of security. I think we have to come to grips with the fact that the end of the ages, which the Christian church must face, is upon us. It is to be a time of great trouble and trial for Christianity.

Now, I am not going to argue about the pretribulation, midtribulation, or posttribulation positions; or whether Jesus is coming before the tribulation, in the middle of the tribulation, or after the tribulation. I have a dear friend who claims he's a pantribulationist: Everything is going to pan out in the end! I think he's probably closer to the truth than he knows.

> *The whole world is going to hell on the doorstep while we're fighting about nothing!*

We've been so busy fighting amongst ourselves. We are so busy arguing about whether or not Christ is going to come before the tribulation, in the middle of the tribulation, or after the tribulation—which is pure *trivulation*, anyhow! Premillennial, aumillennial, postmillennial. Sprinkle them, pour 'em, immerse 'em. Give 'em wine, grape juice, or Coca-cola at the communion service; leavened bread, unleavened bread. Bishops, ruling elders, deacons; no bishops, no ruling elders, no deacons. Back and forth, in and out, up, down. . . . The whole world is going to hell on the doorstep while we're fighting about nothing!

We *must* get our minds off peripheral theology and get down to the main business of the church—which happens to be how to penetrate the world. Many people awaiting the second advent of Jesus Christ do nothing for the kingdom. They're so heavenly minded they're no *earthly* good, and this is exactly what we want to avoid.

―೧ ೧―

Something to Think About

Are you lost in peripheral theology?

O the years in sinning wasted.
Could I but recall them now,
I would give them to my Savior,
To His will I'd gladly bow.

Must I go, and empty-handed?
Must I meet my Savior so?
Not one soul with which to greet Him:
Must I empty-handed go?
―"Must I Go, and Empty-Handed"

―೧ ೧―

Something to Do

Take a moment and reevaluate your life. What can you do to penetrate the world?

28

Be Bold!

I eagerly expect and hope that I will in no way be ashamed, but will have sufficient courage so that now as always Christ will be exalted in my body, whether by life or by death.

—Philippians 1:20

The apostle Paul wrote that courage—boldness—should be a perpetual way of life—always. The word *boldness* doesn't mean what we think it means today. Boldness isn't intellectual or physical arrogance.

Boldness should be a way of life.	Boldness isn't snobbery; the "I know something you don't know, you poor thing" attitude. Do you know some Christians actually talk that way to people in the cults? By the time they get finished with them, the people

are humiliated. They don't even want to talk anymore, they're so hurt.

We forget sometimes that *people* are not our enemies. Our warfare is not against flesh and blood, but against the spiritual rulers of the darkness of this age (Eph. 6:12). That's the war; that's the battle—not the people. They're just pawns in the chess game of satanic conception.

Boldness should be a way of life. It is putting on the whole armor of God and standing against the methods of the devil. If we resist him, he will flee (James 4:7). But we've got to *resist*. We've got to stand up and be counted.

—◦ ◦—

Something to Think About

Boldness is putting on the whole armor of God and standing against the methods of the devil.

> *Mortals, join the mighty chorus,*
> *Which the morning stars began;*
> *Father-love is reigning o'er us,*
> *Brother-love binds man to man.*
>
> *Ever singing, march we onward,*
> *Victors in the midst of strife;*
> *Joyful music lifts us sun-ward*
> *In the triumph song of life.*
> —"Joyful, Joyful, We Adore Thee"

—◦ ◦—

Something to Do

Remember that *people* are not our enemies. Our warfare is against the spiritual rulers of the darkness of this age (Eph. 6:12).

29

Remember the Glory

As far as the east is from the west,
so far has he removed our transgressions from us.
—Psalm 103:12

Let's not forget what Christ has saved us from—Christians sometimes get the idea that because they are Christians they can forget the past. God doesn't want us to forget what we have been redeemed from; God wants us to remember it. He wants us to forget the horror and remember the glory of redemption.

The only being in the universe that can *will* to forget is God. You can't and I can't, but he can. He says, "I will remember your sins against you no more" (Heb. 10:17). You were

Remember the glory
of redemption.

foolish, you were weak, you were base, you were despised, you were nothing . . . and so was I. But God chose to take these vessels of clay and infuse within them his Holy Spirit, that the excellency of the glory might be of God and not of us; that we might be transformed to the image and likeness of Jesus Christ, so that right at this moment we stand in his presence, just as if we had never sinned—whole and complete.

If you died tonight and stood before the Judge of the universe, he might ask you, "What is your right to heaven? Why should I let you in?" You would have no answer whatsoever, unless you could say, "Jesus Christ and his righteousness." That is the heritage of the saints.

Jesus Christ came into this world to save sinners. God wants you to forget the horror and remember the *glory* of redemption. The old hymn is right—"We touch him in life's throng and press, and we are whole again." Jesus Christ loves you. Accept what you really are as God sees you, and then believe what you can become through the Lord Jesus Christ.

Something to Think About

Jesus has transformed us, so that we may stand in God's presence—whole and complete.

> *I've found a friend, O such a friend!*
> *He loved me ere I knew Him;*
> *He drew me with the cords of love,*
> *And thus He bound me to Him.*
> *And 'round my heart still closely twine*
> *Those ties which can't be severed.*
> *For I am His, and He is mine,*
> *Forever and forever.*
> —"I've Found a Friend, O Such a Friend"

Something to Do

Take a few minutes and kneel before God; *remember* the moment you first asked Jesus into your heart.

30

The Right Words

The fool says in his heart,
  "There is no God."
They are corrupt, their deeds are vile;
  there is no one who does good.
                                        —Psalm 14:1

Some people are very blasphemous and very blatant in their unbelief. They stagger through life saying, "Who's God? Blank, blank, blank. It's my life! I'm going to live *my life*." Have you ever met people like this? I meet them all the time. You can't talk to them, unless the Lord gives you the right words at the right moment. If the Lord gives you the right words at the right moment, you can say everything.

Several years ago, I had some problems trying to move into my new home. It was the middle of winter, we had three small children, and the only thing keeping me from getting into the house was a building inspector who wouldn't come up and inspect it. I pleaded with the people at Town Hall. "I've got to get in there!" I said.

"Well, this guy is a *beep, beep,* and he won't let you in."

"Let me talk to him, *please!*" I asked, in a last ditch effort to do *something*.

So they gave me his telephone number, and I called him at home on a Saturday. It was a very bad day for him. I called him up and said, "Listen, I hate to bother you, but I've got to get my wife and my children into the house. It's winter. We just got the house finished. There's nothing wrong with it; it only needs your Certificate of

Occupancy. Will you just come over for fifteen minutes, look through it, and write out the report so we can move in?"

He was quiet for a second, and then he snapped at me, "I wouldn't come to your house if *Jesus Christ* asked me to!"

You know, you just can't allow such arrogant blasphemy and unbelief to go unchallenged. You must speak out. The Lord gave me exactly the right sentence, then. I would never have thought of it myself. I said, "The time will come when Jesus Christ will not ask you anything; he will *command* you and you will come, because you will be dead!" And I hung up the phone.

> *If the Lord gives you the right words at the right moment, you can say everything.*

He was there in fifteen minutes!

"Good morning, Reverend. Nice to see you. Nice house you have here. Hope you enjoy it."

I never heard a word from him again. That was just the right thing God wanted to get through to him. If he would not listen to Jesus Christ in this lifetime, he would listen to him in the next. Don't be afraid to confront people. If the Lord gives you the right words at the right moment, you can say *everything*.

—◦◦ ◦◦—

Something to Think About

You can't allow arrogant blasphemy and unbelief to go unchallenged.

> At the sign of triumph
> Satan's host doth flee;
> On, then, Christian soldiers,
> On to victory!
> Hell's foundations quiver
> At the shout of praise;
> Brothers, lift your voices,
> Loud your anthems raise!
>
> Onward, Christian soldiers,
> Marching as to war,
> With the cross of Jesus
> Going on before!
> —"Onward, Christian Soldiers"

—◦◦ ◦◦—

Something to Do

Study Proverbs 2:10–15. Ask God for the right words.

31

_ɔ̃ ̃_

Face to Face with God

*In the beginning was the Word, and the Word was
with God, and the Word was God.*

—John 1:1

The Gospel of John and John's writings are paramount in New
Testament teaching, not just because of the simplicity of style and
Greek, but also because of the man's profound grasp of the identity
and ministry of Jesus Christ. I call John's Gospel, John's Epistles, and
the Revelation of John "The Gospel of Eternity"—the good news of
eternity.

Matthew portrays Jesus Christ in the strictly Jewish context as
Messiah, son of David. Mark presents him as the suffering servant of
Jehovah who comes into the world to bring the good news of the
kingdom of God. Luke portrays him in a clinical, austere, magnifi-
cently historical narrative as the Son of Man, who took our form and
bore our sins on the cross.

The Gospel of John is completely different. John's approach to
Jesus Christ is not just as Messiah, not just servant, not just identified
with human flesh; John's portrayal of Christ is the core of
Christianity. John reveals him as the eternal Word of God made flesh;
the wisdom of God come to reside in humankind. John's Gospel, as
well as his first epistle, begins on this high note: In the beginning was
the Word, and the Word was face to face with God, and the Word was
God. John then describes for us something about the nature of the
eternal Word.

It's very significant that John did not begin his gospel, "In the beginning was the Son of God." Please notice this. He did not begin that way. He begins with this enigmatic phrase, "In the beginning the Word was *face to face with God*." The Greek word means "face to face." The Word stood face to face with God—and the Word was God.

Dr. Julius Mantey, who wrote along with Dr. Dana the classic and definitive grammar of the Greek New Testament, was a friend of mine, and he made a very succinct observation about this point. He said, "Walter, if you really want to be deadly accurate in the Greek," and he *had* been for sixty-five years, "translate it this way, 'In the beginning the Word *was*, the Word was *face to face* with God, the Word was *deity*. Jesus is not his own father. Jesus Christ is not his spirit. Jesus Christ is the Word or the wisdom of God himself."

Christ is the core of Christianity.

John Henry, Cardinal Newman, the great Roman Catholic theologian made an observation about John 1 that has never been improved upon. He said, "God calls Jesus of Nazareth 'the Word,' the wisdom of God in human flesh, that we should never forget that he is true deity. There never was a moment when wisdom could be separated from personality. A man's wisdom is connected with his personality. You can't separate them. God's wisdom is connected with God's personality. As God is eternal, so is his wisdom. And so he calls Jesus Christ 'the Word,' the reason or the wisdom of God, so that we might never forget that he always existed united with deity. He calls him his Son, so that we might not think of 'the Word' as an abstract philosophical principle, a theological argument, or a Jewish abstraction."

"The Word" is a *person*, the Word was face to face with God, and the Word was deity.

_⟋ ⟍_

Something to Think About

Jesus is the wisdom of God come to reside in humankind.

> *Bless me, O my Savior, bless me,*
> *As I sit low at Thy feet!*
> *O look down in love upon me,*
> *Let me see Thy face so sweet!*
> *Give me, Lord, the mind of Jesus,*
> *Make me holy as He is;*

> *May I prove I've been with Jesus,*
> *Who is all my righteousness.*
> — "Sitting at the Feet of Jesus"

Something to Do

Review this message and write down the answers to these questions: How did Matthew portray Jesus? Mark? Luke? John? Why are these separate portrayals so important?

32

_⊙ ⊙_

Test Everything!

*Test everything. Hold on to the good. Avoid every kind
of evil.*

—1 Thessalonians 5:21–22

If you run your life by comparing your experiences in spiritual matters to other people's experiences in spiritual matters, and if you
spend your life weighing experience against experience, you are never
going to learn anything. You're supposed to get into the Word of
God, the sound foundation, the immovable block. Once there, with
your spiritual feet grounded in the Holy Scripture, you test everyone
that comes down the pike—no matter who
they are.

*If you can't tell fleece
from fur—lookout!*

You don't condemn them: you love them
for Christ's sake, but you *test* them, because
it's your soul and your mind into which the
poison might go, and if you can't tell the dif-
ference you're in trouble—big trouble. If you don't know the Word of
God well enough to know the difference between the wolves of
destruction and the sheep of God's sheepfold, you are going to be
one confused person. If you can't tell fleece from fur—lookout! You
are a prime candidate for doctrinal corruption.

All the teachers in the Church are to test each other, in the light of
the Word of God, by the history of the Church and her pronounce-
ments on the great doctrines of the Bible. There's no such thing as

instant teaching authority. We are told never to lay hands on people suddenly, nor to exalt novice? Do you know why? Because if they're mixed up in *their* thinking, they may eventually mix up your thinking! I don't care how sweet they are. I don't care how many miracles are attributed to their meetings. I don't care about all of the folderol of publicity kits, television appearances, and the things that go to promote people in the world of religious hustling. I'm only concerned with one thing—Is it scriptural? Will it stand up? If it won't, jettison it. If it will, defend it. But at least have brains enough, determination enough, and confidence enough in yourself, the Word of God, and the Holy Spirit not to let somebody sell you something just because it sounds good.

No doubt my words will be interpreted as hostility. That's right! I am eternally hostile to false teachings—and you'd better be too. Otherwise, they will disrupt your life and the lives of others.

Something to Think About

Is it scriptural? Will it stand up? If it won't, jettison it. If it will, defend it.

> *Leave no unguarded place,*
> *No weakness of the soul;*
> *Take every virtue, every grace,*
> *And fortify the whole.*
>
> *From strength to strength go on,*
> *Wrestle and fight and pray;*
> *Tread all the powers of darkness down*
> *And win the well-fought day.*
>   —"Soldiers of Christ, Arise"

Something to Do

Romans 3:7–8 presents an interesting perspective on this lesson. What did Paul mean?

33

Define Your Terms

For if someone comes to you and preaches a Jesus other than the Jesus we preached, or if you receive a different spirit from the one you received, or a different gospel from the one you accepted, you put up with it easily enough.

—2 Corinthians 11:4

One thing is very sadly missing in the Christian church today: We don't define our terms. We just take it for granted that everyone understands what we're talking about.

That's one of the reasons why the cults have grown so tremendously. A Jehovah's Witness can sound exactly like us, have exactly the same form of godliness, as Paul warns us, yet deny the power or authority thereof. A Mormon is a perfect counterfeit of Christianity. They look like us; they act like us; they sound like us. They tote a Bible, they quote Scriptures, and yet they deny that Jesus Christ is God incarnate and that salvation is by grace as a gift of God. I learned from teaching over the years that it is imperative that we define our terms. When somebody says the word *Jesus,* it means nothing by itself unless it's defined within the context of the New Testament.

They tote a Bible, they quote Scriptures, and yet they deny that Jesus Christ is God incarnate and that salvation is by grace as a gift of God.

The Jesus of the Jehovah's Witnesses is an angel. The Jesus of the Mormons is one god among many gods and the spirit brother of Lucifer, who is the devil. The Jesus of the spiritists is an advanced medium in the sixth sphere. The Jesus of the Theosophists and Edgar Cayce is a reincarnation of the world's soul. The Jesus of the mind science cults is a good man in whom the Christ consciousness dwells, which is the same Christ consciousness they say is in all of us.

So when you use the word *Jesus* itself, you have to remember Paul's words, "a Jesus other than the Jesus we preached, . . . a different spirit, . . . a different gospel. . . ." Counterfeit ministers—deceitful workmen—pervert or change the Word of God. Define your terms. Don't just take it for granted that everyone understands what you're talking about.

Something to Think About

Do you know *why* you believe?

> *Breathe on me, Breath of God,*
> *Until my heart is pure,*
> *Until with thee I will thy will*
> *To do and to endure.*

> *Breathe on me, Breath of God,*
> *Till I am wholly thine,*
> *Till all this earthly part of me*
> *Glows with thy fire divine.*
> —"Breathe on Me, Breath of God"

Something to Do

Who is Jesus, specifically? Can you define your terms and back it up with Scripture?

34

The Nature of the Enemy

But mark this: There will be terrible times in the last days. People will be lovers of themselves, lovers of money, boastful, proud, abusive, disobedient to their parents, ungrateful, unholy, without love, unforgiving, slanderous, without self-control, brutal, not lovers of the good, treacherous, rash, conceited, lovers of pleasure rather than lovers of God—having a form of godliness but denying its power. Have nothing to do with them.

—2 Timothy 3:1–5

This portion of Scripture is seldom preached because it upsets people. And I calculate that any section of Scripture that upsets a number of people *must* be worthwhile, and *must* have a great deal to recommend it.

The spirit of the age in which we live cannot be safely ignored by the Christian church. It is not an age that breathes kindness and tolerance, compassion, understanding, or love. It is an age that brings out the very worst in the character of man. We have been at the end of the ages, according to the apostle John for almost two thousand years, and we are moving forward to the cosmic day of divine judgment. It is not unloving to tell people the truth. You can get into a great deal of trouble for doing it, but if you're in the ministry of God to win popularity contests, you have chosen the wrong place. You are supposed to be a witness for Jesus Christ no matter what it costs, no matter what circumstances face you.

Now, I want to tell you something that may make you unhappy—and after careful consideration, I really don't care. It's the truth. Today the Church is under attack on multiple fronts by atheism, agnosticism, and skepticism. Secular humanism poisons the minds of our children so that we send them to school singing, "All Hail the Power of Jesus' Name," and they come out spouting every kind of false doctrine and teaching imaginable. We have made the mistake of thinking that if we *preach* Jesus Christ, it is not necessary to *defend* his gospel. Let me tell you something: It is a *command* to defend the gospel of Christ.

If you're in the ministry of God to win popularity contests, you have chosen the wrong place.

You must see the nature of the enemies of the gospel: They can look like us, they can sound like us, they can purr like pussycats, they can quote our Bible, but when we get down to the rock-bottom line of Jesus Christ, they will not believe in him! They will oppose the gospel, and they will destroy the flock of God if you do not resist them in Jesus' name.

Something to Think About

It is a *command* to defend the gospel of Christ.

> *Behold how many thousands still are lying,*
> *Bound in the dark prison house of sin,*
> *With none to tell them of the Savior's dying*
> *Or of the life he died for them to win.*
>
> *Give of thy sons to bear the message glorious;*
> *Give of thy wealth to speed them on their way;*
> *Pour out thy soul for them in prayer victorious;*
> *And all thou spendest Jesus will repay.*
>
> —"O Zion, Haste"

Something to Do

We live in an age which brings out the very worst in the character of man. The spirit of this age cannot be ignored. Ask God for wisdom today, and the courage to deal with the enemies of the gospel.

35

Recognize the Challenge

Preach the Word; be prepared in season and out of season; correct, rebuke and encourage—with great patience and careful instruction.

—2 Timothy 4:2

The apostle says, "Preach the Word," whether it's convenient or inconvenient. Some Christians are waiting around for it to become convenient to talk about Jesus. They want to make absolutely certain that no one gets mad at them. When they finally decide to witness, they do it with plastic smiles on their faces, saying, "Jesus loves you, Jesus loves you." They hand out a few tracts, spout a few quotations from the gospel, and tell all about how they've been born again. And when they're all done, they think they've discharged their obligation to God. Well, they haven't. You are supposed to pass out the tracks and give the witness, but it is imperative that you give people reasons for your faith.

There are so many Christians desperately trying to sound good to the world. They are so worried about offending them that they never get around to *preaching* the gospel.

It is imperative that we return to the biblical standard of righteousness. It is righteous to preach Jesus Christ. It is righteous to reprove, to rebuke, and to exhort. It is righteous, it is holy, it is just, and it is good to stand against the Prince of Darkness. And Christians, if they are going to be strong in the Lord and in the power of his might, are going to have to recognize that challenge and respond to it. It is the function of every pastor and every man of God not only to preach the Word and feed the sheep, but to stand up for Christ's sake and *defend* against the wolves, lions, and bears that will destroy the Church if we do not move out against them, in Jesus' name.

Some people say I spend a great deal of my time fighting. I do! But not with the Church. I fight with the *enemies* of the gospel, because that's what we are commanded to do. What do you want to do? Roll over and play dead? Retreat from the Jehovah's Witnesses? Shake your head when the Mormon missionaries pedal by? Forget about the Scientologists and run off to some meeting where you throw your arms into the air and shout, "Hallelujah!" while you let all the filth of earth stay on your doorstep? That's Christianity? No, that's madness. If you're going to be an effective Christian, you must be *filled* with the Spirit and *empowered* by the Spirit to go into the world with *boldness* and speak for Jesus Christ.

> *It is imperative that we return to the biblical standard of righteousness.*

―◌◌―

Something to Think About

It is righteous, it is holy, it is just, and it is good to stand against the Prince of Darkness. You must *respond* to the challenge.

> *Have we trials and temptations?*
> *Is there trouble anywhere?*
> *We should never be discouraged—*
> *Take it to the Lord in prayer.*
>
> *Can we find a friend so faithful*
> *Who will all our sorrows share?*
> *Jesus knows our every weakness*
> *Take it to the Lord in prayer.*
> —"What a Friend We Have in Jesus"

―◌◌―

Something to Do

Have you struggled with indifference? Spend time with the Lord, today, and keep this in mind:

> "The LORD is my strength and my shield;
>   my heart trusts in him, and I am helped.
> My heart leaps for joy
>   and I will give thanks to him in song."
> —Psalm 28:7

36

The Mark of a Believer

"If you love me, you will obey what I command."
—John 14:15

Jesus said the first thing you're going to do if you love me—if you're truly, genuinely a believer—is *obey* me. The acid test of the presence or absence of love is the presence or absence of obedience.

Does that mean that Christians are always obeying, all of the time? No! The Lord has already made provision for our sins. The mark of a believer is a life that follows Christ's commands. If you say you love him, and your life is one continuous disavowal of that love: If your mouth is dirty; if your mind is dirty; if your ethics are corrupt; if your morality is rotten; if all you've got is a vocabulary of redemption and you do not have the fruit of redemption, which is *transformation,* you're a tare in the wheat field. You look like us, you sound like us, you sometimes act like us, but you are not one of us. The mark of the believer is to obey Christ as a way of life.

> The mark of the believer is to obey Christ as a way of life.

Again, it does not mean that you *always* obey, because we're sinners saved by grace. But it means that your way of life is a life ordered by obedience to Christ. Love of Christ ensures obedience to Christ. Obedience to Christ ensures the love of the Father. The love of the Father ensures that he, in Christ, dwells with us. The mark of regeneration is a life of obedience, and your life grows stronger and more

perfect in that obedience as you yield yourself daily to the Holy
Spirit.

―⟡ ⟡―

Something to Think About

The acid test of the presence or absence of love is the presence or
absence of obedience.

> *All to Jesus I surrender,*
> *All to him I freely give;*
> *I will ever love and trust him,*
> *In his presence daily live.*

> *All to Jesus I surrender,*
> *Lord, I give myself to thee;*
> *Fill me with thy love and power,*
> *Let thy blessing fall on me.*

> *I surrender all, I surrender all,*
> *All to thee, my blessed Savior,*
> *I surrender all.*

> —"I Surrender All"

―⟡ ⟡―

Something to Do

Study Galatians 5:22–25. Commit verses 22 and 23 to memory.

37

Why Don't You Believe?

"You are the light of the world. A city on a hill cannot be hidden. . . . Let your light shine before men, that they may see your good deeds and praise your Father in heaven."
—Matthew 5:14, 16

I'll never forget what happened years ago when I was living in New York City. While finishing my graduate studies at New York University, I worked a sales job that required rather strange hours. I worked from 6:30 P.M. until 2:30 A.M., and then I went back to classes again the same day. The hours were odd, but the job was great. I loved it. Eventually, I finished all the courses I could take on that schedule, and I thought for sure I'd lose the job—which was paying for my courses. I thought, *What am I going to do now, Lord?* I knew he would take care of things; I just had no idea of how he would go about doing it.

Soon after I had prayed, the man who headed up the department called me into his office and said, "I understand you're thinking about changing jobs."

"I have to change," I explained. "I need to work in the daytime now because of my school schedule." He smiled and told me about an opening on the day shift. *Wonderful,* I thought, and I took the job.

During my lunch hour, I would go down to the corners of Wall Street, Broad, and Nassau, a kind of juncture where there was a Federal Reserve building in the heart of Manhattan's downtown financial district. Everyday, somewhere between two hundred and five hundred people of every conceivable kind of theological and philosophical persuasion congregated. There was also a small core of street preachers who regularly came down to that corner, planted their flags, set up their boxes, and fearlessly preached Jesus.

The discussions were always interesting, but the preachers would inevitably run into trouble when someone interrupted with a tough question. The question would come at the worst possible moment, and they'd get sidetracked from the gospel message. Certain people loved going from preacher to preacher, throwing questions at them just to shut them up. It was the marketplace of Athens or Ephesus all over again.

It was the market-place of Athens or Ephesus all over again.

Well, one day I got all the street preachers together and suggested, "Brethren, I have a lunch hour at approximately the same time you preach. Let's coincide my hour with yours, and if people ask you questions you can't answer, just ship them over to me. It'll get them out of the crowd, and if I don't know the answers, I can stall them long enough for you to finish the sermons. I'll try to come up with answers by the next day." Everyone agreed.

So the next day we went out, and they got up on their boxes while I stood over by the subway entrance with my back against the building. The hecklers came as usual and started going from group to group, but now the preachers could say, "Hey! We've got a guy who can answer your questions." I would be breathing prayers at this juncture. "He's right over there." Pretty soon, about 150 people had me pinned against the wall. We were blocking the subway exit, and a policeman actually came and stood next to me to make sure I wasn't taking bets!

Well, there was one fellow that came out every day. He had a Ph.D. in chemistry and worked for one of the big corporations. He was well-read, immaculately dressed, well-spoken, and a real gentleman. He'd come over while all the people were heckling, yelling, and swearing at me, and sooner or later he'd get up to the front of the group. That's when the fun would begin—he always had some good chestnuts to chew on. He must have done his homework every night.

After my first or second encounter with him, I knew I was in over my head. I couldn't possibly come up with answers to everything, so I asked the Lord, "*Please,* if I can't answer him completely, at least give

38

Don't Ever Do That Again!

Miriam and Aaron began to talk against Moses because of his Cushite wife, for he had married a Cushite. . . . The anger of the Lord burned against them, and he left them. When the cloud lifted from above the Tent, there stood Miriam—leprous, like snow. Aaron turned toward her and saw that she had leprosy.

—Numbers 12:1, 9–10

Moses married a woman with dark skin, and Miriam and Aaron— who were very high-ranking people in the theocracy of the time— spoke against Moses. And so God turned Miriam *white* with leprosy as a mockery—a cosmic joke. He said, "You don't like black women? I'll make you a very white one." There is nothing whiter than leprosy. Miriam had to repent. She was put outside the camp and brought back in again seven days later, and God healed her after Moses prayed.

Now, what does that tell you about God? He doesn't look at the color of skin! He only sees one color—red: the sacrifice of his Son on the cross. He doesn't see race, and he never forbids the races to inter-marry. The problem of racial intermarriage is a cultural problem, not a biblical problem. We should be concerned with what God thinks of this, and God doesn't approve of this attitude. Remember Miriam when you start thinking about discrimination against races. God doesn't like it, and he spit in Miriam's face.

You may ask, "How do you know that?" Because when God was talking to Moses, he said, "If her father had spit in her face, would she not have been in disgrace for seven days? Confine her outside the camp for seven days; after that she can be brought back" (Num. 12:14). The leprosy of Miriam was the spittle of God. He spit on her and put her outside the camp and said, "Don't you ever do that again!"

If God doesn't like something, there's no sense in irritating him.

From that time on, the record shows that Miriam never, ever discriminated against Moses and his wife. A very healthy thing to keep in mind is this: If God doesn't like something, there's just no sense in irritating him.

Something to Think About

God doesn't look at the color *of skin. He only sees one color,* red*: the sacrifice of his Son on the cross.*

> *For my pardon this I see—*
> *Nothing but the blood of Jesus;*
> *For my cleansing, this my plea—*
> *Nothing but the blood of Jesus.*
>
> *Oh! Precious is the flow*
> *That makes me white as snow;*
> *No other fount I know,*
> *Nothing but the blood of Jesus.*
>   —"Nothing but the Blood"

Something to Do

Read Numbers 12. What can be learned from this terrible mistake?

39

The Future Belongs to God

*Pharaoh said to Joseph, "I had a dream, and no one
can interpret it. But I have heard it said of you that
when you hear a dream you can interpret it."*

*"I cannot do it," Joseph replied to Pharaoh, "but
God will give Pharaoh the answer he desires."*

—Genesis 41:15–16

What does Satan first try and do in the doctrine of the demons? Make
Jesus *a way*, but not *the* way. Secondly, he is engaged in trying to get
people absorbed with the future. That is the second plank in this doctrine. Look at Acts 16. What was this girl involved in? Soothsaying.
Do you know what a soothsayer is? A soothsayer is not a psychiatrist,
not a psychologist, not a pharmacist. A soothsayer is somebody who
predicts the future.

The person who wants to interpret the future apart from God is a
person who would lead you away from the
Lord your God. And that person is dangerous,
no matter who they are; whether they wear a
cross around their neck or not. Crosses are
cheap, and pious talk is cheap. What really
counts is whether or not you have any substance to faith and reality to experience,
whether or not you have been to the cross
and have been touched by the hand of the
Lord Jesus. It is possible to be in the Church, baptized, teaching

> *The person who
> wants to interpret
> the future apart
> from God is a person
> who would lead you
> away from the Lord
> your God.*

Sunday School, married to a Christian, and living the whole bit out in the open, and to be filled with every kind of unclean spirit, if you have never been to the cross. There are people like this in our churches and all around us, and we wonder why the Church is powerless. Why? Because Christians have no discernment. Is it any wonder that the Scripture tells us in 1 Corinthians 12 that one of the great gifts of God's Spirit is to some, the discerning of the spirits? We must be able to tell what we're dealing with, and God has not left us in darkness.

I cannot help but think of Genesis 40 in this connection. Joseph, who was a prophet of God, was given this illumination by the Holy Spirit. This is what God had to say on the subject, "Do not interpretations belong to God?" (Gen. 40:8).

The only reliable source of information on the future is the Word of God. Any attempt to gain information from any other source is not only dangerous, but in direct contradiction to the teaching of Scripture. The future belongs to God. Don't play with it.

_⌐☉ ☉⌐_

Something to Think About

Review the first two planks in the doctrine of the demons:

1. Jesus as *a* way, not *the* way.
2. Get people absorbed with the future.

> *My heart has no desire to stay*
> *Where doubts arise and fears dismay;*
> *Tho some may dwell where these abound,*
> *My prayer, my aim is higher ground.*
>
> *Lord, lift me up and let me stand*
> *By faith on heaven's tableland;*
> *A higher plane than I have found—*
> *Lord, plant my feet on higher ground.*
>
> —"Higher Ground"

_⌐☉ ☉⌐_

Something to Do

Remember how the enemy's strategy works and be on guard against it.

40

Spectators or Players?

Therefore put on the full armor of God, so that when the day of evil comes, you may be able to stand your ground, and after you have done everything, to stand.
—Ephesians 6:13

Are we really taking what God says seriously? He says, "Correct, rebuke and encourage" (2 Tim. 4:2). What does *correct* mean? It means saying to someone, "You are wrong." What does *rebuke* mean? "You ought not to do this: You should do this." What does *encourage* mean? "Come and do it this way." That's what the Christian is committed to: correcting, rebuking, and encouraging or exhorting.

There will be hostility on the part of the world. Today we are trying to please the world and the Lord, and we are not going to make it. John the Baptist came neither eating nor drinking; he was an abstainer, and they called him a lunatic and cut off his head. Jesus Christ came and participated, and they labeled him "a glutton and a drunkard, a friend of tax collectors and 'sinners'" (Matt. 11:19). John the Baptist, the greatest of the Old Testament prophets, could not please the world by abstinence and Jesus Christ could not please the world by participation. How do you think you're going to please it either way? You can't. Therefore, since we can't please the world, we had best be prepared to please God.

> Today we are trying to please the world and the Lord, and we are not going to make it.

The crisis in which we find ourselves today is a crisis of conflict, in which God has called us to put on the whole armor and to stand against the forces of darkness. If we don't recognize the forces of darkness, we can't stand against them. If we don't recognize Satan's power, we will ignore it. If we do not know what is happening in the world, we can become apathetic and lackadaisical. But if we know the world in which we live, and we know that these are the last times, and we know the nature of man, and we know that Christ is the answer to the ultimate question of eternal destiny, then we can enter into the conflict.

We can't be like football players warming the bench and cheering the team on. We have to be participants! It has been well stated, and truthfully so, that the person who does not participate in the crises of his or her time has never really lived at all. For if we do not participate, we are not actually living it. We are spectators.

What has God called you and me to be? Spectators or players? There are those who *watch,* and those who *put on* the armor of God and go forth to war.

<hr>

Something to Think About

You may be committed to Christ, but are you committed to his service? Which are you—spectator or player?

> *Fight the good fight with all thy might!*
> *Christ is thy strength, and Christ thy right;*
> *Lay hold on life, and it shall be*
> *Thy joy and crown eternally.*
> —"Fight the Good Fight"

<hr>

Something to Do

The crisis in which we find ourselves today is a crisis of *conflict,* in which God has called us to put on the whole armor and to stand against the forces of darkness. Examine Ephesians 6:10–18 from this perspective. Ask for wisdom and strength to stand.

41

The Mess Is Ours

For the secret power of lawlessness is already at work;
but the one who now holds it back will continue to do
so till he is taken out of the way.
—2 Thessalonians 2:7

Don't call into question God's attributes of mercy and compassion. Call into question the mess that we made of the earth in which we live. When God created it, it wasn't intended to be this way. The beauty that's in the world was God's idea. The mess was ours. And now, when we look around and see a world cursed by sin, and we see judgment in that world—concentration camps, holocausts—we blame God.

Why do these things take place? Because man has the freedom to sin and God has the freedom to deal with it when he chooses to do so. He dealt with sin once and for all on the cross of Jesus Christ.

You must understand the sinfulness of sin. The sinfulness of sin gives you a world cursed by sin. Why do nice Christians get cancer?

You must understand the sinfulness of sin. Why do nice Christians have automobile accidents and die? Why do faithful servants of God get struck down on the left and on the right? Because we are all under the judgment of sin (Rom. 3).

You live in an imperfect world. You are aging. You were born aging. You can't restore a perfect world. You can't go back to Eden.

The world is all about the process of disintegration—the curse of sin. It's not an oversimplification. God says that.

So yes, there are tragedies. Yes, children die at an early age. Yes, people die suddenly. Yes, there are all kinds of sufferings. The important lesson to learn from it is this: We're making choices, we've made choices, and the world is the result of those choices. But now things are different; we can make choices *for God* and ask him to deliver us from these things . . . and many times he will.

If you only knew the number of times you've been spared sickness. If you only knew the times your life has been spared. One time I sat down and tried to remember all the times I was close to death, as an unbeliever and as a believer. I looked back on it and said to myself, "How great is the mercy and compassion of God that he could take care of me so many times when I was certain to be killed or to die."

You live in a cursed world, but if God were *not* intervening in it— you think you've got problems now? You think the world's got problems? If God did not intervene in the world, you'd see much more evil than you could possibly dream of right now. So be grateful for the small percentage of evil.

Don't ever look at and doubt the attributes of God, the character of God, or what God did and *why* God did it. Take a good long look in the mirror at the mess we made of it, then say, "Thank you, Lord, Sovereign of heaven and earth, that you have been merciful and gracious and kind—and we are still alive." It is very unsafe to debate the character and attributes of God in his presence.

—⟊ ⟊—

Something to Think About

The sinfulness of sin gives you a world cursed by sin. Don't call into question God's attributes of mercy and compassion.

> *Jesus calls us: by thy mercies,*
> *Savior, may we hear thy call,*
> *Give our hearts to thine obedience,*
> *Serve and love thee best of all.*
> —"Jesus Calls Us O'er the Tumult"

—⟊ ⟊—

Something to Do

The next time someone blames God for this mess, tell them who's *really* responsible.

42

_⌒ ⌒_

Put God to the Test

*Do not be anxious about anything, but in everything,
by prayer and petition, with thanksgiving, present
your requests to God. And the peace of God, which
transcends all understanding, will guard your hearts
and your minds in Christ Jesus.*

—Philippians 4:6–7

There are a number of ways to ascertain the will of God. Prayer, of
course, is very important. Ask God to do something specific—Gideon
called it a fleece.

I remember when I first considered coming to California. My
ministry remained strong in the eastern part of the United States, and
I had not ventured too much into the western

*How do you find the
will of God?*

part. It became very clear to me at that time
that God wanted me to move to the West
Coast. But I didn't want to go, because I was
quite comfortable where I was.

So I kept putting it off and refusing to consider it, until one day a
man walked into my office. He smiled as he sat down and said, "I
think you have a very good voice for taping. I'd like to put you on
tape and expand this ministry, if you're interested."

Surprised, I answered, "Yes!"

He continued, "I live in California, and I'd like you to do the
taping in California."

All of a sudden a little light went on in my head and I thought, *Ah ha—an opportunity to put a fleece out. Lord, if you want me to come to California, boy is this one going to be tough for you!* I was going to give him a real cruncher.

I said, "You'll need to book me in the meetings."

He seemed rather surprised. "I'm a missionary and a business man. I don't go around booking people."

"You want me in California?" I asked. "You book me in at least three places. I'll come out, and you can record me at those places, and see if I can do the job."

"All right!" He agreed, "If that's what it takes, we'll do it."

I secretly told God, "If you want me to go, this man will book me. The meetings will be enormously successful, and everything will work out perfectly the way you want it to. If I see that, I'll move."

Well, the man who was going to book the meetings left for Mexico and dropped it in the lap of someone else. Sometime later the new guy called me and said, "I don't know how to go about doing this, Walt," (I thought, *I'm not going to California!*) "but, I went ahead and booked three churches anyhow."

I was speechless!

This is how God does things: He booked me into a Presbyterian church, an Episcopal church, and a Quaker church! How's that for a cross section?

I said, "OK, we'll see how it works out."

I flew to California, and there were no arrangements for honorariums. No contracts were signed between us. I didn't know what would happen. It seemed like a disaster; they hadn't even advertised the meetings, because they didn't know how to go about doing it. I thought, *This is going to be a busteroo for sure! This fleece is going to come up absolutely bone dry.*

At the first meeting, the cars were lined up for eight blocks, and the people were wall-to-wall and standing in the aisles! When I finished, they roared their approval and clapped. They'd been reading my books. I thought, *This is remarkable. Praise the Lord!* And even the offering was very substantial.

Well, I went to the Episcopal church. It was a small church but jammed full of people. We had a wonderful time. They were charismatic Episcopalians, and I really got blessed in my spirit. I couldn't argue with that one. The offering was as big as the Presbyterian church, with a third of the people.

Finally, I visited the last one, the Quakers. I felt sure I'd win there, but La Mirada Friends Church was wall-to-wall people, and they were even outside the windows, sitting in chairs on the patio! When I finished speaking I said to God, "OK, I'll put you to the test now." So I told the congregation, "I've been praying about coming to California and bringing Christian Research out here. I haven't even talked it over with my board yet, but how would you feel about something like that in California?"

The people gave me a standing ovation for five minutes. They shouted at me from all over the building, "Come! Come!"

I came.

I knew the will of God. The ministry increased a thousand percent. Every door opened, and no one shut it. That was the hand of God.

How do you find the will of God? You can do many things. Persist in prayer and fasting, study his Word, and persist in laying fleeces before the Lord. That's how I found out the will of God—I asked God to do something, and he did it.

Something to Think About

God wants you to come to him.

> *I hear the Savior say,*
> *"Thy strength indeed is small,*
> *Child of weakness, watch and pray,*
> *Find in me thine all in all."*
>
> *Jesus paid it all,*
> *All to him I owe;*
> *Sin had left a crimson stain,*
> *He washed it white as snow.*
>
> —*"Jesus Paid It All"*

Something to Do

When Gideon needed direction, he went to the Lord with two requests. Study Judges 6:36–40 in the light of Jeremiah 29:11–13. Remember—God will answer *you* too.

43

Don't Be Discouraged

> *Therefore, since we have such a hope, we are very*
> *bold.*
>
> —2 Corinthians 3:12

The key to witnessing in the kingdom of the cults is this: You must run the risk of being hated by the very people you are talking to, that they may be born again! If you're willing to do that, God will give you fruit. I just want to tell you, don't be discouraged!

When I began writing my first book, I looked around for literature to do a bibliography, and it didn't exist. I searched for articles and couldn't find *anything*. I had to tramp through all of these cultic head-quarters collecting information for a library. I filled up a room full of material, which I then distilled into the book. Without this kind of research you cannot make an impact on the mind of the kingdom of the cults.

So don't get discouraged. God is tearing up the kingdom of the cults! Mormons and Jehovah's Witnesses are getting saved. The chief overseer of Jehovah's Witnesses in Great Britain—twenty-six years as a Jehovah's Witness—gave his testimony at my Bible class. He got saved! And he's been leading Jehovah's Witnesses out so fast the Watchtower's having a hemorrhage! Of course, they've been predicting the end of the world for so long, it's a wonder they have *anybody* believe them anymore. They've come to be known as "Armageddon, Incorporated!"

Don't be discour-
aged!

If you don't think that something's happening, you've been asleep. Things are happening. Don't be discouraged!

—⸂ ⸃—

Something to Think About

You must run the risk of being *hated*. If you're willing to do that, God will give you fruit.

> *Work, for the night is coming,*
> *Work thro' the sunny noon;*
> *Fill brightest hours with labor,*
> *Rest comes sure and soon.*
>
> *Give every flying minute*
> *Something to keep in store;*
> *Work, for the night is coming,*
> *When man works no more.*
> —"Work, for the Night Is Coming"

—⸂ ⸃—

Something to Do

Praise God and thank him today for the souls he will bring to Christ through you.

44

_⸪ ⸫_

I'm Just Grateful . . .

When the woman saw that the fruit of the tree was good for food and pleasing to the eye, and also desirable for gaining wisdom, she took some and ate it. She also gave some to her husband, who was with her, and he ate it.

—Genesis 3:6

We live in a world that is subject to our choices, as well as to the sovereignty of God. It was man who chose to fall by rebelling against God. It is man who continues to make exactly the same choices in rebelling against God—insisting he has the right to sin and not suffer the consequences. That's nonsense!

God can never win in this kind of a debate, and I'll tell you why: If God intervenes and stops all evil dead in its tracks right now, then people will begin to shout, "Where is our right to make choices? We don't have any freedom of choice. That's not fair!" If God intervenes and stops all the murders and all the evil in the world, it's not fair, because now we can't make any choices. But if God says, "OK, you made your bed—lie in it. But when it pleases me, I'll turn the covers over myself," then we complain, "Why don't you do something about this? You're all-powerful, why don't you intervene and stop this?" So either way, God can't win. Therefore, the argument is a waste of time.

> It was man who chose to fall by rebelling against God.

110

We live in a cursed creation, and we have chosen to live in it. We are suffering the results of it. I'm just grateful that God restrains evil as much as he does now.

―◌ ◌―

Something to Think About

Man continues to make exactly the same choice in rebelling against God—insisting he has the right to sin and *not suffer the consequences.*

> *Father-like He tends and spares us,*
> *Well our feeble frame He knows;*
> *In His hands He gently bears us,*
> *Rescues us from all our foes.*
>
> *Praise, my soul, the King of Heaven,*
> *To His feet thy tribute bring;*
> *Ransomed, healed, restored, forgiven,*
> *Evermore His praises sing.*
> —"Praise, My Soul, the King of Heaven"

―◌ ◌―

Something to Do

"This day I call heaven and earth as witnesses against you that I have set before you life and death, blessings and curses. Now choose life, so that you and your children may live and that you may love the LORD your God, listen to his voice, and hold fast to him" (Deut. 30:19–20).

Hide this word in your heart.

45

_ꢰ ꢰ_

A Great Secret Truth

*Where is the wise man? Where is the scholar? Where
is the philosopher of this age? Has not God made foolish the wisdom of the world? For the foolishness of
God is wiser than man's wisdom, and the weakness
of God is stronger than man's strength.*
                                    —1 Corinthians 1:20, 25

One Sunday morning someone in my Bible class asked me this question: He'd just begun studying philosophy in school, and he couldn't
understand why his philosophy professors didn't appear to be very
rational or logical. Well, he was right. They're not rational and they're
not logical in many things.

I took my B.A. in philosophy and my master's degree under
Dr. Sidney Hook at New York University. Dr. Hook was a disciple of
John Dewey, the greatest enemy of Christianity we've had in the last
hundred years in the United States. I know all the reasons why I
should be an agnostic and all the reasons why I should be an atheist—
and they're all a crock of garbage! They're just a cover-up for your sins.

Let me show you how far they'll go. Dr. Hook was one of the most
brilliant philosophers in the world. I took specific notes in his class,
and one day a student asked Dr. Hook, "What would you accept as
absolute proof of the existence of God? How do you deal with the
problem of God yourself, personally?"

Dr. Hook answered—in my class, in my hearing, with my eyes fas-
tened on him—"If I were to die and wake up in the presence of

Jehovah, I would be able to give him logically consistent arguments as to why I did not accept his existence when I was on the earth." That's a direct quote!

So yours truly, old troublemaker, raised his hand and asked, "Dr. Hook, Sir," (he was a formidable teacher) "wouldn't the fact that you woke up and God was there destroy all your logical arguments?"

"Ahhhhh, well," he replied, "you have to understand that I live essentially by the laws of formal logic. I believe in logic as a means of truth."

"That isn't the point." I argued, "The point is that if you wake up and he's there, you were wrong. All your logic is wrong. The fact that he's there proves it." Well, he rambled off on something else, and I never got an answer.

What kind of ego is it that thinks it can wake up in the presence of an infinite intellect—who knows all arguments as *conclusions*—and discuss logic? He knows everything as a basic premise before you even open your mouth! He knows what it is, what you're going to say, and where you're going with it. How could you wake up in his presence and claim, "The reason I didn't believe in you is logically demonstrable." God would say, "Fascinating. I'm here, aren't I? You're here, aren't you? One of us isn't thinking straight—and it certainly isn't me!"

Logic?

I'll tell you something about the philosophers that they don't normally discuss. I learned this after about ten years of study in the field. Here it is—ready? A great secret truth: All schools of philosophy, almost without exception, refute their predecessors so as each new school arises, the next school refutes it. And they just keep going on and on in this everlasting cycle of drivel, refuting each other.

They have never built a hospital; they have never built an old age home. They have made no contributions whatsoever to the social welfare of mankind. They are parasitical individuals who live off the festering carcass of education and unbelief. "That's exactly what they are." They argue all the time in their own defense. They're always defending their sins.

―∞ ∞―

Something to Think About

God knows everything as a basic premise before you even open your mouth!

In haunts of wretchedness and need,
On shadowed thresholds dark with fears,
From paths where hide the lures of greed,
We catch the vision of thy tears.
　　—"Where Cross the Crowded Ways of Life"

Something to Do

Contemplate the "foolishness of God" as you consider 1 Corinthians 1:18–31.

46

_⟳ ⟲_

Our Ancient Foe

*You, dear children, are from God and have overcome
them, because the one who is in you is greater than
the one who is in the world.*

—1 John 4:4

The New Testament teaches a personal satanic being. The New
Testament teaches that evil beings, or spirit beings, control individuals; that they are capable of creating illness—mental and physical;
that they are capable of binding people; that they are capable of creating all forms of symptoms in human life; and that, unrecognized,
they can wreak awful destruction.

Some people feel it's fashionable to ignore the fact that there's such
a thing as demonology in the Bible, or that there is such a thing as the
genuine and the truly important study of demons in the Old and the
New Testaments. But anyone who has any knowledge of occultism or
the kingdom of the cults knows immediately how foolish this is.
Demons are not little individuals running around in red union suits
with pitchforks—copies of the devil and a caricature of him that he
loves to see the world make, particularly on Halloween. Demons are
instead, malignant beings who are simply other-dimensional: They
live in a dimension other than ours, but they are capable of entering
this dimension.

The Scripture says there are other dimensions. The Bible tells us
about the dimension of heaven, the throne of God. Quite obviously,

it is not here. The Lord Jesus Christ ascended through the heaven-lies—through dimensions into the heaven of heavens.

Then there is the dimension mentioned in Scripture which is populated by Satan, prince of darkness, god of this age, ruler of this world. He is here and his representatives are here. The New Testament gives graphic illustrations of their presence and their power. For us to come to grips with them, we must first recognize there is such a thing as the dimension of Satan and the existence of demons. The New Testament reveals it to us (Eph. 6:12). So we know there is the visible heaven we can see here with the stars, planets, and galaxies; there is a dimension beyond this under the control of the prince of the powers of the air; and beyond that dimension is the throne of God.

The Bible tells us that, if not for the direct intervention of God the Holy Spirit, the Church would be overcome by the power of Satan (2 Thess. 2:6), but it is the Spirit that restrains it right now. That is why John exalts in 1 John 4:4, "You, dear children, are from God and have overcome them, because the one who is in you is greater than the one who is in the world." We are protected by the person, the presence, and the power of the Holy Spirit.

We are protected by the person, the presence, and the power of the Holy Spirit.

In the New Testament, what precise evidence do we have for demons? I think the best example I can cite is Jesus Christ. We know that when Christ encountered the demons early in his ministry, he dealt with them. They are fallen angels, fallen spirits who followed Lucifer in his rebellion against the throne of God. They worshiped him, not God. They are quite literally Satan's children. When Christ encountered them, he dealt with them. And they confessed something about him: "What do you want with me, Jesus, Son of the Most High God?" (Mark 5:7). When Christ encountered them, he expelled them.

When he encountered Satan, he did not encounter the *corporate evil* within man; he did not encounter *philosophic abstraction*; he was not simply using *personification* to speak of evil. When Jesus encountered the devil, he had a dialogue with him. Either Christ was schizophrenic—which the New Testament flatly rejects as do we—or he was speaking with another dimensional being. In this conversation with Satan, Satan revealed something: "Again, the devil took him to a very high mountain and showed him all the kingdoms of the world and their splendor. 'All this I will give you,' he said, 'if you will bow down and worship me'" (Matt. 4:8–9). Satan desires *worship*.

Now, a demon isn't lurking behind every lamppost and under every seat, but it is very foolish to assume there are none at all. This is precisely what the world has assumed and why we are in the condition we are in right now. This great force is loose. We are busily trying to give it other names, but we will not succeed.

They are here. They are real. They are powerful. If we ignore them, we do so at our own peril.

_ɕ ɕ_

Something to Think About

When Jesus Christ encountered evil, he dealt with it.

> *A mighty fortress is our God,*
> *A bulwark never failing;*
> *Our helper he, amid the flood*
> *Of mortal ills prevailing:*
> *For still our ancient foe*
> *Doth seek to work us woe;*
> *His craft and power are great,*
> *And, armed with cruel hate,*
> *On earth is not his equal.*
> —"A Mighty Fortress Is Our God"

_ɕ ɕ_

Something to Do

Take a few moments and commit 1 John 4:4 to memory. Reflect on the *immense power* promised to you in this verse.

47

_⌒ ⌒_

He's Alive!

*The angel said to the women, "Do not be afraid, for
I know that you are looking for Jesus, who was cruci-
fied. He is not here; he has risen, just as he said.
Come and see the place where he lay."*
—Matthew 28:5–6

How do you know that Christianity is the true religion? I know
Christianity is the true religion because the Scriptures have been val-
idated in my mind beyond a question of a doubt. Jesus Christ is the
centerpiece of the Scriptures, and I accept the testimony concerning
him.

In addition to this, I have had an existential encounter with Jesus
Christ in which I have *met* him. I know from archaeology; I know
from history; I know from the validity of the text of Scripture; I know
from the person of our Lord; I know from the
Holy Spirit; and I know from personal experience. Those are very good reasons *why.*

*The difference
between the rest of
the religious leaders
of the world and
Jesus is this: They're
dead. He's alive!*

You see, the difference between the rest of
the religious leaders of the world and Jesus is
this: They're dead. He's alive! The whole New
Testament is based on the fact that he is risen.
If he didn't rise from the dead as he claimed
he would, no one would have believed in
him. They would have labeled him a false prophet.

Do you remember what the Jews said when Jesus died on the cross? They wanted to put a watch on the tomb because the "deceiver" said he would return in three days. Pilate gave them their watch. They sealed the tomb with a Roman seal (Matt. 27:63–66). The soldiers were there—and the angel of the Lord rolled away the stone—and *Jesus Christ wasn't there.* They have never recovered from the initial impact of that shock almost two thousand years ago. They're still trying to babble their way out of it, but they're not going to do it.

He's alive! I know because I pray for people week after week in the name of Jesus Christ, and they're healed. Dead saviors don't heal anyone.

Something to Think About

How do you know that Christianity is the true religion?

There is no name so sweet on earth,
No name so dear in heaven,
As that before his wondrous birth
To Christ the Savior given.

And when he hung upon the tree
They wrote his name above him,
That all might see the reason we
Forevermore must love him.

We love to sing of Christ our King
And hail him blessed Jesus;
For there's no word ear ever heard,
So dear, so sweet as Jesus.
—"There Is No Name So Sweet on Earth"

Something to Do

Praise God today for his marvelous gift.

48

Children of God

Your love has given me great joy and encouragement,
because you, brother, have refreshed the hearts of the
saints. Therefore, although in Christ I could be bold
and order you to do what you ought to do, yet I appeal
to you on the basis of love. I then, as Paul—an old
man and now also a prisoner of Christ Jesus—I appeal
to you for my son Onesimus, who became my son
while I was in chains. Formerly he was useless to you,
but now he has become useful both to you and to me.
I am sending him—who is my very heart—back to
you.

—Philemon 7–12

Philemon has only twenty-five verses in it, but it contains one of the most beautiful of all stories on how God deals with the sins of men. If you want to know how he does it, Philemon gives you the blueprint.

Paul writes this letter to Philemon, but it's not only addressed to him—the Church itself is also intended as the recipient. Paul is addressing a personal problem, but he wanted the Church as a whole to learn the proper treatment of slaves. If you read the passage very carefully you will find that he's talking about a runaway slave.

Philemon was not only a believer; he was a generous Christian who also owned slaves, which was legal in the Roman Empire. He must have been well-off to be a slaveholder, and clearly he was well-liked. Paul said that he "refreshed the hearts of the saints" by his giving and by his testimony. Paul tactfully approached Philemon with the attitude of friendship. He in essence says, "Look, I'm not going to come at you with a divine command as an apostle of Jesus Christ. Rather, I'm writing this to you as a brother and as a friend." He implores Philemon as an "old man" in chains.

Now, here's a man who knows how to get to you. What did he really mean? "I appeal to you. I'm writing this letter on behalf of someone else." This is an *intercessory* letter.

Onesimus was a runaway slave, an offense punishable by death in the Roman Empire. Paul was in prison, and Onesimus was a slave in prison awaiting the sentence of death because he had run away from his master. He was chattel, a piece of property. But Paul writes an intercessory letter for a slave, which was unheard of in those days. It was one thing to write an intercessory letter for a free man or to write one for a friend; that was acceptable decorum. But to write a letter for a man branded as worthy of *death* was an extraordinary act on the part of the apostle Paul. It was the direct opposite of Judaism and everything he had learned in his culture. He broke down all the cultural barriers when he said, "My letter to you, Philemon, is to intercede for someone the State considers worthy of death—and maybe you do, also."

Paul sent Philemon an "update," so to speak, on the man who was once "unprofitable." Paul wanted him to know that Onesimus had *become* profitable to Paul—and he hoped Onesimus would be profitable to Philemon also. Onesimus is being released from prison to face possible death, and Paul wanted to emphasize that Onesimus is now bound to him—Paul—with spiritual chains that bind him far more than any physical chains. He is Paul's spiritual *child*, and he asks that Philemon receive him as such.

An interesting parallel may be drawn here to the Lord Jesus Christ. Christ has begotten us to a new and a living hope through his resurrection from the dead. We are his children, united to him by faith. Even though we are *physically chained* because of sin in the world; even though we have an anchor, our physical body, which holds us to this earth, an anchor only death can wave; even though physical slavery still exists in the world today, the chains of the gospel bind tighter than all chains that men can forge. The chains of the gospel bind us to Christ as Onesimus was bound to Paul—inseparably. St. Augustine once said, "He is only truly free, who is the slave of God."

When Paul uses this line of reasoning, he actually means, "God saved Onesimus and bound him to himself with the chains of eternal love. I want you to learn something from his running away, as he has learned. He ran away from slavery and became the slave of God. I'm sending back to you not just any old runaway slave, doomed under Roman law. I'm sending back to you my *son.*" He wanted Philemon to receive Onesimus back as he would have loved and received Paul back.

> *"He is only truly free, who is the slave of God."*

Can you read between the lines, here? Paul pleads, "Set him free! Free him, as you should free all your slaves." Dr. Frank Gaebelin once pointed out to me a beautiful picture in this small epistle. It cannot be erased. It is the picture of God receiving us because of Jesus Christ: God overlooking our rebellion, our running away, and our unprofitableness, and taking us because of the Lord Jesus. Paul went so far as to take upon himself any debt Onesimus might owe. Jesus took upon himself every debt we ever owed.

The Epistle to Philemon is the "Gospel of Emancipation." It's the good news that God has set the prisoners free. This little epistle goes out to the Church and says between the lines, "Behold, how much the Father loved you that you should be called sons of God—slave or free."

Something to Think About

We are God's children united to him by faith.

> *Tell of the cross where they nailed him,*
> *Writhing in anguish and pain;*
> *Tell of the grave where they laid him,*
> *Tell how he liveth again.*
> *Love in that story so tender,*
> *Clearer than ever I see:*
> *Stay, let me weep while you whisper,*
> *Love paid the ransom for me.*
> —"Tell Me the Story of Jesus"

Something to Do

Carefully read the Book of Philemon and see how much the Father loves you.

49

Never a Moment of Doubt

"You diligently study the Scriptures because you think
that by them you possess eternal life. These are the
Scriptures that testify about me, yet you refuse to
come to me to have life."

—John 5:39–40

Ionochada, a friend who was one of the most gifted philosophy students at New York University, scored in the upper one percentile of all philosophy students in the United States—an inconceivably brilliant mind. He used to needle me ruthlessly every chance he got because I was a theist: I believed in God. We'd go at it time and time again.

One night, as we sat in the cafeteria drinking coffee, we had a very interesting discussion. I'll never forget it; it's as if it took place yesterday morning. His name was Kaye. We chatted back and forth for a couple of minutes, and he started needling me again. Finally, I said to him, "Kaye, tell me what you think of Jesus of Nazareth, honestly."

He answered, "Jesus of Nazareth was an extraordinary human being. He had fantastic insights into the minds of men and into their motives. I've read the New Testament, and I'm very impressed with the person of Jesus." *This* from a Jewish philosophy student!

"Good!" I continued, "Do you think Jesus was essentially a truthful person?"

"Jesus of Nazareth was an extraordinary human being."

123

"Oh, I don't think there's any doubt about that at all," he replied.

"Would you say that Jesus was, perhaps, the greatest moralistic teacher you've ever read?"

"Oh, I don't think I'd doubt that for a minute, either. I've read all of them."

"I'm so glad to hear that," I stated. "Now, if you were me, knowing you as I do: hopping from bed to bed, boozing, swearing, telling dirty jokes, living exactly the way you want to live; if you were me, would you listen to *Jesus* on the existence of God, or *you?*"

He looked at me for a minute, put his coffee cup down, and answered, "If you put it that way, I think I'd listen to Jesus."

"There never was a moment of doubt. *Never,*" I said.

A few weeks later in class, we were arguing vigorously again with the professor refereeing, when all of a sudden Kaye spouts off, "Now just a minute!" (I thought, *Oh boy, now I'm going to get it!*) But this time he said, "Martin and I are poles apart. We know our differences of opinion here, but you know, he does have a valid argument. His valid argument is on the *person* of Jesus. I don't hear anyone here saying they're equal with Jesus. Anybody here think they are? No? Well, that's Martin's position—until you are, *shut-up!*"

Kaye and I became friends. We drank coffee regularly, and I "gave it to him" every chance I got. So you see, the Lord uses little things . . . even a cup of coffee.

—◌◌—

Something to Think About

Our valid argument is on the *person* of Jesus Christ.

> *Thou camest, O Lord, with the living word*
> *That should set Thy people free;*
> *But with mocking scorn,*
> *And with crown of thorn,*
> *They bore Thee to Calvary.*
>
> *O come to my heart, Lord Jesus,*
> *There is room in my heart for Thee.*
> —"Thou Didst Leave Thy Throne"

—◌◌—

Something to Do

Go to God in prayer and ask him to use a "little thing" in your life to reach someone today.

50

Talk to Me

Who foretold this long ago,
  who declared it from the distant past?
Was it not I, the LORD?
  And there is no God apart from me,
a righteous God and a Savior;
  there is none but me.
  —Isaiah 45:21

One of the most successful of all demonic teachings is this: Play with what you have no power over. Why? Because it turns you away from him who has the power to control all things, into whose hands we must commit ourselves as witnesses and servants of Jesus Christ.

Isaiah 45, is a very telling passage. Here, the prophet spells out for us in clear terms what God wants us to know.

> **What does God say? "Talk to me about it!"**

What does God say? "Talk to *me* about it!" Don't talk to crystal balls. Don't talk to bearded prophets. Don't talk to people who claim they can read your palm. Don't talk to people who read the tea leaves. Don't talk to people who can tell you all things about everything because they have the answers. "Talk to me," says the Lord. Why? Here are his credentials: "It is I who made the earth and created mankind upon it. My own hands stretched out the heavens; I marshaled their starry hosts" (Isa. 45:12).

How does God answer the people who are always trying to find out about the future? "Talk to me about it. If you really want answers,

I have them. And if I don't want to give them to you, it's better that you don't know them." If you knew everything that the future held right now, maybe you wouldn't want to go home tonight; maybe you couldn't look at the person next to you, or that member of your family; maybe life wouldn't be bearable anymore. That's why the Lord has placed these things within his own providence.

Something to Think About

The first three planks in the doctrine of the demons are:

1. Jesus is *a* way, not *the* way.
2. Get people absorbed with the future.
3. Get people to play with what they have no power over.

What does God say? "Talk to *me* about it!"

> Trust in Him, ye saints, forever,
> He is faithful, changing never;
> Neither force nor guile can sever
> Those He loves from Him.
>
> Keep us, Lord, O keep us cleaving
> To Thyself, and still believing,
> Till the hour of our receiving
> Promised joys with Thee.
>
> —"Praise the Savior"

Something to Do

Search your heart today. Can you say this and mean it?

> "But I trust in you, O LORD;
> I say, 'You are my God.'
> My times are in your hands."
> —Psalm 31:14–15

51

The Power of God

As I urged you when I went into Macedonia, stay there in Ephesus so that you may command certain men not to teach false doctrines any longer nor to devote themselves to myths and endless genealogies. These promote controversies rather than God's work—which is by faith. The goal of this command is love, which comes from a pure heart and a good conscience and a sincere faith.

—1 Timothy 1:3–5

I did something a few years ago that hadn't been done before: I traveled to Salt Lake City, and I invited the professors of Brigham Young University, along with the leaders of the Mormon church, to attend some meetings downtown at First Baptist Church. I offered to answer any and all questions on Mormonism they might want to ask. I was coming not as a Baptist minister, but as a full professor of comparative religions, with all the necessary credentials.

You couldn't get near that church for four blocks! It was jampacked. Mormon missionaries came; two apostles attended. It was a madhouse. I lectured and then I answered questions. No apostle stood up. No bishop stood up. The *missionaries* stood up. The leadership sat on their hands while the young people got massacred—*in love.*

Afterward, two Mormon missionaries came up to me with a man they were trying to convert. They shook hands with me and said, "We enjoyed your presentation. It was honest. If the church is ever to be destroyed, it will be by what you are doing. You used our own material! How can we say anything against our own material?"

When God destroyed Goliath of Gath, he didn't do it with the stones. He cut off his head with his own sword! The twitching corpse of Mormon theology will lie still one day because its head was cut off by its own archives. It will happen in God's own, dear providence.

There is no stopping the power of God!

The next week, those two missionaries came forward in that First Baptist Church and were born again. There is no stopping the power of God!

Something to Think About

God will destroy any Goliath who dares come against him. Are you willing to be David?

> *My life, my love I give to Thee,*
> *Thou Lamb of God who died for me;*
> *Oh, may I ever faithful be,*
> *My Savior and my God!*
> —"I'll Live for Him"

Something to Do

Read about David and Goliath in 1 Samuel 17. What made David unique?

52

No Contest

*Do you not know that your body is a temple of the
Holy Spirit, who is in you, whom you have received
from God? You are not your own.*
— 1 Corinthians 6:19

A dangerous teaching is loose in the Church today. Many Christians
have been victimized by it, and, therefore, it must be examined and
thoroughly eliminated.

The New Testament knows nothing of demon possession of
Christians. It does not teach it! If the Spirit of God dwells within us,
and Jesus said he would abide with us forever, then I have to con-
clude that the Christian is exempt from demon possession. However,
we are *not* exempt from demon influence. Use whatever terms you
like: *oppression, fascination*—I have half a dozen descriptors of what
can take place in a fascination with evil and with satanic power—but
none of them is possession.

Possession is demonization, in which the individual does not
have the *capacity* to deal with it any longer. So, when a person is truly
demonized they are beyond any help whatsoever, except divine help.
I know because I've conducted enough exorcisms to recognize and
understand demon possession. It is an extremely terrible and evil
experience to have to undergo. It does *not* happen to Christians.

I know people who say, "But I know an example. . . . I remember
this. . . . I see this. . . ." I've seen a lot of these things, too, but this is
an experience that should be tested by the Scriptures. The Scriptures

should not be interpreted by the experience. Test all experience by Scripture, not the reverse! Until I see biblical evidence for demon possession of Christians, I'm not going to accept *anyone's* testimony on the subject. I ask people all the time to "produce the evidence." They cannot.

Test all experience by Scripture.

Demonic *oppression,* however, works in quite a number of ways. If you yield yourself and become the servant of sin (Rom. 6), you become its slave. Demonic power can influence you if you have yielded yourself to sin. The way demonic oppression takes place is that you lose your interest in the study of the Scriptures, you lose your desire to be a witness, and you lose the yearning for fellowship with other members of the body of Christ. Your prayer life virtually disintegrates. And if the demons are really after you, and you have yielded yourself to sin, then they can interfere with your psychological profile, with your thinking processes, and pretty generally wreak havoc in your life. Now, every time something like this happens to you does *not* mean it's demonic oppression, but these are characteristics that can go along with it.

If you are born again, you cannot be demon possessed because the Holy Spirit lives inside of you. Your body becomes his temple. If the devil knocks on the door, the Holy Spirit answers—and it's *no contest!*

―◌ ◌―

Something to Think About

If you yield yourself and become the servant of sin (Rom. 6), you become its slave.

> *Down in the valley*
> *with my Savior I would go,*
> *Where the storms are sweeping*
> *and the dark waters flow;*
> *With His hand to lead me*
> *I will never, never fear,*
> *Danger cannot fright me*
> *if my Lord is near.*
>
> —"Follow On"

―◌ ◌―

Something to Do

Do not allow your heart to be overcome by fear! God will deliver you and strengthen your walk with him. Just ask!

53

True Believers

> *It is impossible for those who have once been enlightened, who have tasted the heavenly gift, who have shared in the Holy Spirit, who have tasted the goodness of the word of God and the powers of the coming age, if they fall away, to be brought back to repentance, because to their loss they are crucifying the Son of God all over again and subjecting him to public disgrace.*
>
> *—Hebrews 6:4–6*

Many Christians live in fear, constantly worrying that something they may do or say will cause them to "lose" their salvation. I always deal with this question of "losing" salvation by pointing out a sound biblical answer to it.

In this passage, every single thing mentioned could be said of Judas Iscariot. He was a perfect tare in the wheat field. He wasn't really a believer—he was a perfect counterfeit. He went along with the Holy Spirit, he used the name of Jesus to heal, he preached the gospel of the kingdom of God, he sat at the table of the Lord—you name it—Judas was the perfect counterfeit. *But he was never saved.* If you looked at him, you would say, "There's a believer," but he was never a believer. Jesus said, "Have I not chosen you, the Twelve? Yet one of you is a devil!" (John 6:70). If you consider all these things about Judas that fit this passage, then it is clearly dealing with *counterfeits*—with the bad ground that in the end produces corrupt fruit, but looks for all the world like the real thing.

If you read other people's writings in this area, they may argue that Hebrews 6 teaches that you may lose your salvation, *and you may not be able* to be renewed to repentance. The

People backslide all over the place, but they come back . . . because they are true believers.

only problem is, the passage says it is *impossible* to renew the ones who have fallen away to repentance. People backslide all over the place, but they come back. It is not impossible to renew them to repentance, because they are *true believers*. Those who are not true believers, who look as if they are the real thing but they are not—these are the ones who cannot be renewed to repentance.

—◦◦◦—

Something to Think About

God is not the author of fear.

> 'Tis the promise of God
> full salvation to give
> Unto him who on Jesus,
> His Son, will believe.
> Tho the pathway be lonely
> and dangerous too,
> Surely Jesus is able
> to carry me through.
>
> Hallelujah, 'tis done!
> I believe on the Son;
> I am saved by the blood
> of the Crucified One.
>   —"Hallelujah, 'Tis Done!"

—◦◦◦—

Something to Do

Study John 3:16. Rest in the promise of God.

54

Cheer Up!

"If the world hates you, keep in mind that it hated me first. If you belonged to the world, it would love you as its own. As it is, you do not belong to the world, but I have chosen you out of the world. That is why the world hates you."

—John 15:18–19

It is significant that Christ says Christians should anticipate the hatred, the opposition, and the persecution of the world. Is Jesus trying to create a religious paranoia in us? No, he's trying to teach us that if we walk with him, the servant is not greater than his Lord.

If they persecuted Christ, they're going to persecute us. If they rejected his Word, they're going to reject our word. He's trying to fortify us against becoming discouraged when the world hates us. When

> *The servant is not greater than his Lord.*

that happens, we're liable to say, "Is there something wrong with me? Am I the kind of personality that stirs up bad feelings among people? Am I the kind of person that people just love to hate?" Christ is freeing us from that straitjacket. He says, "Cheer up—because if the world does hate you, remember it hated me first. It rejected me before it rejected you." If it rejected incarnate perfection and incarnate love; if it rejected God himself in human flesh—you shouldn't be too upset if it rejects you.

Jesus loved the world completely despite their rejection of him. You and I can't do what Jesus did. He loved them enough, even in the midst of their hatred, to die for the sins of all mankind. When people persecute you, when people speak all manner of evil against you falsely, and it's for *his* sake, remember how they persecuted the prophets before you. You are no different than anyone else who has tried to live a godly life in Christ Jesus. Persecution is the norm for the Christian.

Something to Think About

If they persecuted Christ, they're going to persecute you. If they rejected his Word, they're going to reject your word.

> *I suffered much for thee,*
> *More than thy tongue can tell,*
> *Of bitterest agony,*
> *To rescue thee from hell;*
>
> *I've borne it all for thee,*
> *What hast thou borne for me?*
> —"I Gave My Life for Thee"

Something to Do

God has something to say about popularity: "Woe to you when all men speak well of you" (Luke 6:26). Examine your life in the light of his opinion.

55

Half the Truth

*Someone might argue, "If my falsehood enhances
God's truthfulness and so increases his glory, why am
I still condemned as a sinner?" Why not say—as we
are being slanderously reported as saying and as some
claim that we say—"Let us do evil that good may
result"? Their condemnation is deserved.*

—Romans 3:7–8

A leader of a home Bible study once reprimanded a member of the
group when he dared to criticize a prominent Christian leader for his
error on a doctrinal issue. He felt one Christian brother should not
attack another, and he concluded, "It doesn't matter *how* you bring
one to Christ, just that you *do.*"

How do you scripturally refute this idea that the end justifies the
means? You don't. You can't, because if you will do *anything* to get
somebody to Christ, then why not lie to them? Why tell them the
truth at all? Why not tell them there is no hell? Why not tell them anything you want to tell them, just as long as they inevitably get saved?

No. Scripture teaches specifically that the end does *not* justify the
means. The apostle Paul makes that quite
clear when he writes, "Some claim that we
say—'Let us do evil that good may result'?
Their condemnation is deserved."

> *Scripture teaches
> specifically that the
> end does not justify
> the means.*

A host of ministers today give you half the
truth, part of the truth, and seldom ever *all* of

135

the truth. The reason for that is they don't want to offend anyone. Why? Well, it would cut down on their audiences, and it would certainly cut down on their support. So they won't do it.

You needn't be concerned that you are attacking a brother in this situation. Scripture teaches that every minister is subject to the Church and to Scripture. If he will not accept the discipline of the Church, and will not live within the context of biblical theology, then he is to be reprimanded for it. If he won't listen, he is to be disciplined for it. If he refuses discipline, he's to be excommunicated for it. (See Matt. 18:15–18.) It's as simple as that. Sadly, we have enough in this particular minister's theology to have excommunicated him years ago on the basis of the doctrine of man, the doctrine of eternal punishment, and many other points of doctrine.

What bothers me is that every time you open your mouth as a Christian and pronounce, "This is wrong," you've got some pious person popping up and saying, "Oh, but that's *judgmental*." I don't think they've ever read Paul's first Epistle to the Corinthians, where he says we are *supposed* to judge within the body (5:12–13). If we don't judge within the body, how is anyone ever going to know the truth? People can say whatever they want to say.

You are not attacking a brother if you are holding him accountable. Every minister is subject to Scripture and to the Church, and we must tell people the whole truth—not just a part of it. The end does not justify the means.

—◌ ◌—

Something to Think About

We *must* judge within the body. Scripture teaches that everyone is subject to the Church and to Scripture.

> *A charge to keep I have,*
> *A God to glorify,*
> *Who gave His Son my soul to save,*
> *And fit it for the sky.*
>
> *Arm me with jealous care,*
> *As in Thy sight to live;*
> *And O thy servant, Lord, prepare,*
> *A strict account to give.*
>
>   —"A Charge to Keep I Have"

Something to Do

1 Corinthians 5:6-7 says, "Don't you know that a little yeast works through the whole batch of dough? Get rid of the old yeast that you may be a new batch without yeast—as you really are."

What is the "yeast" Paul is referring to and how can this be applied to the Church today?

56

I Chose You

"You did not choose me, but I chose you to go and bear fruit—fruit that will last. Then the Father will give you whatever you ask in my name."

—John 15:16

This is a tremendous statement of the sovereignty of God. "You did not choose me, but I chose you." The choice of God is obviously based upon certain qualifications and certain factors which are unknown to us. God does not arbitrarily, in eternity, see all mankind and say, "Eeny, meeny, miny, moe, these are the ones to heaven will go!" and the rest are going to hell. That is not the way the mind of God works. That is not divine sovereignty.

Divine sovereignty takes into consideration whatever events, whatever actions, and whatever choices a person is somehow involved in. In other words, there is an interrelationship between the sovereign will of God and the freedom that he has granted to his creation. He retains his sovereignty, man retains the degree of freedom God gives, and there is no conflict between the two.

There is an interrelationship between the sovereign will of God and the freedom he has granted to his creation.

You may say, "But I don't understand that!" No, you do not understand that, and you couldn't understand that unless you were God—or unless God specifically gave you the information. Unfortunately, he hasn't done that. He has never explained predestination, he has never

138

explained foreordination, and he has never explained election or the relationship of free will to any of those. That is not explained anywhere in Scripture. God left it in the area of the *crucible of faith.*

Jesus said we would not understand what he is doing now, but we would understand afterward. So the wise Christian waits until afterward, and doesn't spend his or her time chasing their predestination posterior throughout their entire life. That's like a dog running around in circles after a can tied to its tail. You can run around in circles for the rest of your life trying to solve the riddle of predestination, but you are not going to do it. I have been that route myself. Calvin, Armenias, Luther, Zwingli, and many others could not solve it, which means there's an inaccessibility of data.

"All you have to know," says God, "is this: You didn't choose me, I chose you." There is some basis on which God made the choice, but the fact that we don't understand the basis doesn't mean that we're robots; it doesn't mean that God is some kind of sovereign king who decides whatever he wants to do and takes nothing into consideration. That is not true. That is not the God of the Bible.

In short, the knowledge of how God chooses resides only in the mind of God. You and I can rejoice that he loved us, that he extended that love to us in Jesus Christ, and we responded to it. We did not respond just by our own will, but by an interrelationship between our will and his choice that *no one* has ever been able to untangle.

―♋ ♋―

Something to Think About

The knowledge of how God chooses resides only in the mind of God.

> Ye chosen seed of Israel's race,
> Ye ransomed from the fall,
> Hail Him who saves you by his grace,
> And crown Him Lord of all;
> Hail Him who saves you by his grace,
> And crown Him Lord of all.
> ―"All Hail the Power of Jesus' Name"

―♋ ♋―

Something to Do

Rejoice today in the knowledge that he chose *you.*

57

Get Me Out of Here!

Brothers, I could not address you as spiritual but as worldly—mere infants in Christ. I gave you milk, not solid food, for you were not yet ready for it. Indeed, you are still not ready. You are still worldly. For since there is jealousy and quarreling among you, are you not worldly? Are you not acting like mere men?

—1 Corinthians 3:1–3

In this epistle the apostle Paul accuses the Corinthians of all kinds of carnality, but he still refers to them as "beloved." They are brothers and sisters who have fallen into sin. If you fall into sin and you stay in it, that is proof you are not a believer. The true nature of the believer is to resist sin and not to practice it.

It's like the analogy of the pig and the lamb. If a pig falls into a pool of filth, the pig rolls over in it and stays there because it has no pores, and the cold mud gives the pig some relief from the heat. The nature of the pig is to stay cool and to seek out whatever will help it do the job. But if a lamb comes along and falls into the mud, the lamb cries out for help and struggles to escape. Why? Because the lamb, fully equipped with pores, says, "I don't need this egg foo yung!" The lamb wants out, right?

The nature determines it. If you're a pig by nature, you'll wallow in sin and you won't care. If you're a lamb and you fall into it, you'll feel so rotten and

God always hears us.

140

miserable that eventually you will cry, "Get me out of here!" And thank God, he always hears us.

—❧ ❧—

Something to Think About

The believer resists sin and tries not to practice it.

Abide with me: fast falls the eventide;
The darkness deepens;
Lord with me abide:
When other helpers fail, and comforts flee,
Help of the helpless, O abide with me!

I need thy presence every passing hour:
What but thy grace can foil the tempter's power?
Who like thyself my guide and stay can be?
Thru cloud and sunshine, O abide with me!

—"Abide with Me"

—❧ ❧—

Something to Do

Read and consider carefully Paul's instructions in 1 Corinthians 3.

58

Playing Games

Hide your face from my sins
and blot out all my iniquity.
Create in me a pure heart, O God,
and renew a steadfast spirit within me.
Do not cast me from your presence
or take your Holy Spirit from me.
Restore to me the joy of your salvation
and grant me a willing spirit, to sustain me.
—Psalm 51:9–12

I'd rather judge myself and get right with God, as Paul teaches, than I would have God judge me. That is something you want to avoid at all costs.

Remember, something happened to you when you accepted Jesus Christ as your Savior that never happened before. You were purchased with a price, the precious blood of Christ. Since that means you are not your own, your will—your life— *must* be subject to the will of God. If you think you're going to play games with God after he sent Christ to die for you, lookout! Judge yourself first and don't ever ask God for justice—never, please, not for yourself. Ask him for mercy.

> **You were purchased with a price, the precious blood of Christ.**

If you're having a tough time with someone else, and if you really want the worst possible thing for a person who's wronged you, say,

142

"Lord, deal with him justly." Let that be your prayer. Believe me, he does a much finer job than any of us ever could. Get your heart right with God, and leave other people to him.

—◌ ◌—

Something to Think About

You are not your own. Your will—your life—must be subject to the will of God.

> Breathe, O breathe, thy loving Spirit
> Into every troubled breast!
> Let us all in thee inherit,
> Let us find the promised rest;
> Take away our bent to sinning;
> Alpha and Omega be;
> End of faith, as its beginning,
> Set our hearts at liberty.
> —"Love Divine, All Loves Excelling"

—◌ ◌—

Something to Do

Review the Scripture at the beginning of today's lesson. Take it to heart and make it your prayer.

59

Make God Happy

Shout for joy to the LORD, all the earth.
  Worship the LORD with gladness;
  come before him with joyful songs.
Know that the LORD is God.
  It is he who made us, and we are his;
  we are his people, the sheep of his pasture.
Enter his gates with thanksgiving
  and his courts with praise;
  give thanks to him and praise his name.
For the LORD is good and his love endures forever;
  his faithfulness continues through all generations.
                    —Psalm 100:1–5

When I was a young boy attending the Episcopal church, I remember singing "Old Hundreth": "Praise God, from whom all blessings flow; Praise Him, all creatures here below; Praise Him above, ye heav'nly host; Praise Father, Son, and Holy Ghost." I never look at Psalm 100 without thinking of that hymn of praise.

What better way to begin a new day than to offer God something he likes; to offer God something that makes him happy; to offer God something that you know he accepts because he said so? We try to please God in our lives, many times because we have sinned—and rather than confess that sin to God we proceed to do all kinds of good works to "make up" for the sin. On the outside chance that you might be like this, it's nice to remember that the way to please God involves repentance and restoration. God says in Psalm 50:23, "He who sacrifices thank offerings honors me, and he prepares the way so that I may show him the salvation of God."

If you want to make God happy, offer him the sacrifice of praise. If you want to make God hysterically joyful, *then correct your way of life.* The Hebrew means here, "He changes his way of life." God says, "To that person who praises me and repents, I will show my deliverance."

If you want to make God happy, offer him the sacrifice of praise.

Offer God praise! Not because he is some super-deified megalomaniac who likes to hear day and night, "I love you, I love you. Praise you, thank you, glory to God. Hallelujah!" No, the praise of God is for the benefit of *man.* It reminds us of what he has done for us. You're not benefiting God with some kind of eternal bouquet that he simply can't do without. Through prayer, praise, and thanksgiving, and through the offering of your body as a living sacrifice, you are completing your spiritual worship (Rom. 12:1).

"Shout for joy to the Lord." God doesn't like us going through our Christian lives with our chins dragging on the curbstone. He doesn't want us depressed. He doesn't like us frustrated or feeling like heaven is shielded in brass and we can't get through. All of these feelings are the direct opposite of the peace of God which surpasses all understanding (Phil. 4:4–7). God doesn't intend this for us. What he intends is for us to offer him a sacrifice of praise and thanksgiving, and to come into his presence glorifying him.

Thank him for all the blessings you've seen come about. Obey the Lord—not to make up for your sins—but because he has *forgiven* your sins. Whatever you do, do it gladly. When you forgive someone, forgive him gladly.

How many of you sing to God? Do you sing when you pray? Sometimes, when I'm sitting in a plane, I lean back and start humming hymns. The people next to me may think I'm crazy, but I'm humming, "All Hail the Power of Jesus' Name" and "Holy, Holy, Holy" because they identify Christ in me—the hope of glory. Sing, praise God, come into his presence with thanksgiving. Whatever you do, do it gladly!

_ᴄ⃝ ᴄ⃝_

Something to Think About

The praise of God is for the benefit of man. It reminds us of what he has done for us.

Holy, holy, holy,
Lord God Almighty!
Early in the morning
our song shall rise to thee;
Holy, holy, holy!
merciful and mighty!
God in three Persons,
blessed Trinity!
                    —"Holy, Holy, Holy"

Something to Do

Find a quiet place where you won't be disturbed and offer God the sacrifice of praise. Whatever you do, do it gladly!

60

I Can't Take Anymore!

Do not be anxious about anything, but in everything, by prayer and petition, with thanksgiving, present your requests to God. And the peace of God, which transcends all understanding, will guard your hearts and your minds in Christ Jesus.

—Philippians 4:6–7

God is trying to tell you, "I want to give you peace in your intellect. I want to give you peace in your soul. I want to give you the capacity to *endure.*" No test will come upon us that God will not make it possible for us to endure. He won't permit us to be tested beyond our capacity to resist.

I can say, "Hallelujah!" to that one. So many times I've gotten to the place in my life where I've said, "I can't stand it! I can't take anymore!" How many times have you said, "I can't handle this, Lord"?

"Not to worry," God answers us. "Talk to me about it." We need to remember who made us and who knows us best. We didn't create the little chromosomes, we didn't structure the genes, and we had nothing to do with DNA. Sometimes we think we know so much, but in the essence of it all, we know so very little. God wants to give us peace. John 14:27 promises, "Peace I leave with you; my peace I give you. I do not give to you as the world gives.

God wants to give us peace.

Do not let your hearts be troubled and do not be afraid."

147

We have the gift of peace from God—and it *cannot* be counterfeited. But Jesus did reveal something quite interesting. He said, "My peace I give you. I do not give to you as the world gives." So, it is possible for the world to give peace. It can give peace in terms of money or in terms of being stoned out of your mind on drugs or alcohol. It can give you peace with a sense of security. The world gives all types of peace—but they are not in any way comparable to the peace which surpasses all understanding, which Christ gives (Phil. 4:7).

The peace the world gives is temporal—because the world is temporal and everything changes. But the peace that Christ gives *never changes.* Jesus Christ is the same yesterday, today, and forever, and the person who is born again in the twentieth century may have the same peace as the person in the first century. Why? Because Christ is the Prince of Peace.

Satan may have things that appear to give peace—you may call them counterfeits—but he cannot really duplicate the peace of God. He only has some pretty poor imitations running around the landscape.

When you are in the midst of a test that brings you to your knees, don't be fooled by the enemy. Ask God for his perfect peace in Jesus Christ. When you believe you cannot take anymore—call on him. We are God's people and his sheep. He cares. God wants us to come to him, to trust him, so he may give us rest.

—⟶◌⟶◌⟵—

Something to Think About

You need to remember who made you, and who knows you best.

> *Every joy or trial*
> *Falleth from above,*
> *Traced upon our dial*
> *By the Sun of Love;*
> *We may trust Him fully*
> *All for us to do;*
> *They who trust Him wholly*
> *Find Him wholly true.*

> *Stayed upon Jehovah,*
> *Hearts are fully blessed;*
> *Finding, as He promised,*
> *Perfect peace and rest.*
> > —"Like a River Glorious"

Something to Do

Find a photo of yourself as a small child, and as you look at it, think of this: *You are valuable to God—worth the life of his only Son.* Don't shut God out. Reach for his hand and find peace.

61

A New Command

"A new command I give you: Love one another. As I have loved you, so you must love one another."
—John 13:34

This verse is what I always refer to as the "lost commandment." Why do I call it that? Because it's so absent in the lives of Christians. Now you may say, "I love my fellow Christians. I hug them. I pray for them. I care for them." But just think for a second: Do you love as he loves you?

We need each other in the body of Christ. We need to be fed. We need to share our feelings. We need to be able to confess our faults one to another. We need to learn to love one another as Christ loved us.

I don't mean phony love where everyone hugs you and grabs you and pats you on the back and says, "Glory to God! Hallelujah! I love you!" Sometimes they're patting you on the back just to find a soft spot in which to embed the blade! I've found this to be very true, particularly in some of the circles I've worked in. So I don't go along with all that "sloppy agape." There is nothing wrong with telling someone you love them or giving them a hug or a squeeze on the arm—if you really feel for the person. But don't do it just because it's *expected* of you. That's hypocritical.

There are some people I like that I have difficulty loving. There are people I love that I have difficulty *liking*. Some people neither love nor like me! We all have our problems, but you can't become an icicle when someone demonstrates some form of Christian love toward you. We have to learn to love each other.

Jesus spoke of a quality of love that, when manifested, testifies and convinces the world as nothing else can. It is the love of Christ in us for each other; a far greater love than any kind ever before experienced by mankind. That's why Jesus said, "A new command I give you."

How did he love us? He loved us *unto death*. How did he love us? Vicariously—he was willing to suffer in our place. Do we love each other that way? Do we put other people's interest above our own? Is it what we want or what someone else wants? Is it for the glory of God or for our glory? What is the quality of love you have?

If it's the love of Christ, then it will be a selfless love, a sacrificial love. It will be a giving and enduring love. And if it's the love of Christ, it will be an exemplary love. It will not be something that you put on to impress people. It will be something that flows out of you because Christ is in you. Because he loves you, you are capable of loving each other. Love one another "in the same manner," says the Greek, "as I have loved you."

I believe every Christian—and I, myself, pray to this end—should pray: "Lord Jesus, give me your love, so that I might have *that love* for the body of Christ."

One of the greatest problems with the Church today is that we can't see any farther than our own noses. It's always our *own* denomination; our local congregation; our program; our TV show; our missionaries; our this, and our that—instead of recognizing that the whole body of Christ is *one*. We are to help each other for the cause of Christ. True Christian love transcends all denominational barriers. It goes beyond all sexism and beyond the color of skin. It transcends all normal values. True Christian love transforms us.

True Christian love transforms us.

―――

Something to Think About

What quality of love do you have?

Immortal Love, forever full,
Forever flowing free,
Forever shared, forever whole,
A never-ebbing sea!

O Lord and Master of us all,
Whate'er our name or sign,
We own thy sway, we hear thy call,
We test our lives by thine!
—"Immortal Love, Forever Full"

Something to Do

Philippians 2:1–16 teaches us how to love. Study it carefully with this in mind: "Be devoted to one another in brotherly love. Honor one another above yourselves" (Rom. 12:10).

62

God Speaks

The king said to me, "What is it you want?"

Then I prayed to the God of heaven, and I answered the king, "If it pleases the king and if your servant has found favor in his sight, let him send me to the city in Judah where my fathers are buried so that I can rebuild it."

I went to Jerusalem, and after staying there three days I set out during the night with a few men. I had not told anyone what my God had put in my heart to do for Jerusalem.

—Nehemiah 2:4–5, 11–12

People often wonder how they will know when God speaks to them. Nehemiah talked of how God put knowledge in his heart. I believe that God speaks to our spiritual natures. The heart is a synonym for the soul or for the spirit. I believe God speaks to our hearts very definitively. God tells us things he wants us to do in such a way that we have no rest until we do that specific thing. I can give you illustration after illustration in my life and ministry where the Lord has done that with me.

> *God tells us things he wants us to do in such a way that we have no rest until we do that specific thing.*

I've also had the Lord speak to me through other people. Not too long ago I felt a little bit stressed. I needed to finish writing a chapter of a book coming out, and I had some finishing touches to do on another paperback book. It was a great burden on me with all the other things I'd been doing, and I felt very low in my energy levels. I prayed for the Lord to give me some uplifting word and some guidance. Well, that morning I happened to call Christian Research Institute, and they switched me over to the phone system's background music. There was a man on there preaching *to me* for about two minutes. His text came from Colossians 1:11: "being strengthened with all power according to his glorious might so that you may have great endurance and patience."

I needed to hear that. I needed to be reminded that it didn't depend on my energy; it didn't depend on whipping up my enthusiasm. The Lord's energy is there when I need it. And sure enough, it was. I finished half a chapter!

God speaks through other people in just that way. Sometimes he speaks through a prophetic word in church services. I don't know how many times people have come up to me and said, "That word was meant for *me* this morning." God speaks through circumstances—placing us where we can't *help* but get the message. He speaks to our hearts and, of course, always through his Word. So God speaks to you in numerous ways.

You can be sure that God is speaking to you when the message that comes through is in accordance with the Word of God. It may be for the continuous witness of the individual, the salvation of other people's souls, or the solution to problems you've been praying about. God speaks in remarkable ways.

—◌ ◌—

Something to Think About

The Lord's energy is there when you need it.

> *While walking in the light of God,*
> *I sweet communion find;*
> *I press with holy vigor on,*
> *And leave the world behind.*
>
> —"Sunlight"

—◌ ◌—

Something to Do

Are you struggling with a difficult situation? You have supernatural power available to you. Draw on it! Is confusion clouding your judgment? God will put knowledge in your heart—just like he did for Nehemiah. Pray for it!

63

Itching Ears

*For the time will come when men will not put up with
sound doctrine. Instead, to suit their own desires, they
will gather around them a great number of teachers
to say what their itching ears want to hear. They will
turn their ears away from the truth and turn aside to
myths.*

—2 Timothy 4:3–4

The fourth plank in the doctrine of the demons is: Equate the truth
with mythology. In 2 Timothy 4:3–4, the apostle speaks to the
Church concerning what God expects of Christians and the nature of
the end times. I'm always impressed by these words, because Paul
quite obviously intended that the Church not only be edified by
them, but that the Church communicate them, pass them on, and
prayerfully meditate on them.

What does this passage tell us? At the consummation of time, certain things are going to happen—"They will
gather around them a great number of teachers to say what their itching ears want to
hear." Oh, that's beautiful. That's exactly
what we've got today: Everyone hearing what
they want to hear. Soft lights, soft music, and
even softer sermons characterize our age.

*Soft lights, soft
music, and even
softer sermons char-
acterize our age.*

"They will turn their ears away from the truth and turn aside to
myths." One of the reigning schools of Protestant theology is

Rudolph Bultman's "School of Demythologization." What did Dr. Bultman do? He took all the myths out of the Old Testament and all the myths out of the New Testament. When he finished, he didn't have much of either left. So he *remythologized* the whole thing, and it was worse when he finished than it was before he started. We now have a world with a remythologized New Testament.

The Scripture says, "Lookout!" for one of the doctrines of the demons is to equate the truth with mythology. And that's what we have, the equation of the truth with mythology on every side. Where does it originate? From the freethinkers? From the atheists? From the agnostics? From the skeptics? Oh, no, we're getting it from the theologians—from the seminaries! All the places that should be telling us the truth are giving us the lie that the Bible is mythology, filled with fables and legends that must be reconstructed to meet the needs of our age. *The truth is equated with mythology.*

—◦ ◦—

Something to Think About

Paul intended not only that the Church be edified by this Scripture (2 Tim. 4:3–4), but that the Church communicate it, pass it on, and prayerfully meditate on it.

> *Encamped along the hills of light,*
> *Ye Christian soldiers, rise,*
> *And press the battle ere the night*
> *Shall veil the glowing skies.*
> *Against the foe in vales below*
> *Let all our strength be hurled;*
> *Faith is the victory, we know*
> *That overcomes the world.*
>
> *Faith is the victory!*
> *Faith is the victory!*
> *O glorious victory,*
> *That overcomes the world.*
>
> —"Faith Is the Victory"

—◦ ◦—

Something to Do

Do all of the above—then review the first four steps in the doctrine of the demons:

1. Jesus is *a* way, not *the* way.

2. Get people absorbed with the future.
3. Get people to play with what they have no power over.
4. Equate the truth with mythology.

64

Dangerous Things

In the synagogue there was a man possessed by a demon, an evil spirit. He cried out at the top of his voice, "Ha! What do you want with us, Jesus of Nazareth? Have you come to destroy us? I know who you are—the Holy One of God!"

"Be quiet!" Jesus said sternly. "Come out of him!" Then the demon threw the man down before them all and came out without injuring him.

—Luke 4:33–35

I cannot help but think, when we talk about occultism, just how deadly it can become. Some time ago while giving a series of lectures in New York, a clergyman and his wife came to me with an incredible story. He began, "I have to tell you something because I know you'll believe me. If I tell other people, they'll just write me off."

I said, "Well, after twenty years of seeing all the things I've seen, yes, I think I might just believe you. What happened to you?"

He gave the following account:

> We come from a family of spiritists. Everyone in our family practiced mediumship and held séances. I accepted Christ as my Savior and escaped, but my sister still practiced it. She used the Ouija board and went through the whole routine. I grew so concerned about her that one night I drove to her home. On the way

there, I said to my wife, "Tonight is the night we face her with this."

We arrived and stepped inside, and she was sitting there with a Ouija board on the table. I warned her, "I've come here to show you this thing is devilish."

She just laughed at me. So I sat down across from her, and the two of us started a dialogue with the Ouija board. (Parker Brothers manufactures the "game" Ouija by the hundreds of thousands.) And as I sat there in that room, an eerie feeling came over me. I started to ask questions of the Ouija board—and it answered me.

"Who are you?" I demanded.

The force answered, "S-P-I-R-I-T."

"What is your name?" I continued. It refused to give it.

"Were you there when the resurrection of Christ took place?"

The answer came on the board, "Y-E-S."

"What did you experience?"

"F-E-A-R."

I began to get very concerned., "What do you feel toward me?"

"H-A-T-E."

"What do you think of the Bible?" It spelled out a four-letter obscenity.

At that point, I decided to break off contact with the Ouija board. So I stood up from the table, took my Bible and stated, "I'll have no more to do with this. It's devilish." And I threw my Bible into the center of the Ouija board.

At that moment the board levitated off the table, flipped the Bible into the air, across the room, and into the wall. My sister and my wife screamed. As I stood there watching, something smashed me in the stomach and knocked me to the floor. I doubled over, breathless, with my head between my knees, and the only thing I could gasp was. "Jesus, Jesus, Jesus, help!"

My sister said, "Really, you've gone too far now. You're not going to try and fool me anymore." Still, my position on the floor convinced my wife and sister to come over to help me. When we pulled up my shirt, we saw a red welt the size of a fist over my solar plexus.

At that juncture, my sister recognized that I had been hit—but by nothing visible in that room. The next thing I knew we were all having a prayer meeting. My sister came out of the occult to Christ, and the Ouija board was splintered and burned.

"I never would have believed this, Walt, unless I lived through it. What do you think hit me?"

"Well, read the Book of the Acts," I answered. "The seven sons of Sceva probably had the same question. Remember how they tried to cast out demons? What happened? The demon said, '"Jesus I know, and I know about Paul, but who are you?" Then the man who had the evil spirit jumped on them and overpowered them all. He gave them such a beating that they ran out of the house naked and bleeding'" (Acts 19:15–16).

"I've learned my lesson," he replied. "I leave the Ouija boards and all of this to the Holy Spirit. I don't bother with it anymore."

These are not innocent things. They are dangerous things—but things we must face as believers in Christ.

The people who play with Ouija boards and think it's cute; the people who try to levitate tables; the people who want to read tarot cards, tea leaves, and their palms; the people who are always trying to find out their horoscope—these are the people who are flirting with the kingdom of the occult. And it is *dangerous*, because it reaches out to another dimension and endangers the soul. You don't have to go to Africa to find demons. Africa, South America, the dark continents of the world—none are darker than America.

> *These are not innocent things. They are dangerous things—but things that we must face as believers in Christ.*

—∙୧ ୧∙—

Something to Think About

What can we learn from this man's experience?

> *O how the world to evil allures me!*
> *O how my heart is tempted to sin!*
> *I must tell Jesus, and He will help me*
> *Over the world the victory to win.*

I must tell Jesus! I must tell Jesus!
I cannot bear my burdens alone;
I must tell Jesus! I must tell Jesus!
Jesus can help me, Jesus alone.
　　　　　　　—"I Must Tell Jesus"

Something to Do

Examine Ephesians 6:10–18. What protection does God offer us?

65

No Excuse

"If I had not come and spoken to them, they would not be guilty of sin. Now, however, they have no excuse for their sin."

—John 15:22

This is one of the most interesting statements in all of New Testament theology, yet many people read it and don't catch it. Jesus states that if he had not come and spoken to the Jews, they would not have been charged with accountability for rejecting him and for rejecting the truth of the gospel. But now that he did come, now that he had a discourse with them, they no longer have any excuse for their sin. In other words, sin was not imputed to their account until they *received knowledge* of who he was and what he came to do.

At that moment they were charged with responsibility. They had no cloak for their sins. No more could they say, "But we didn't *know!*" Jesus said, "You did know! I did works among you that no one else ever did. I healed the sick. I raised the dead. I cast out the demons. I preached the gospel to the poor. I opened the eyes of the blind, the ears of the deaf, the mouths of the dumb. I did things no one ever did in the history of the world, and I did it in front of *this* generation! You no longer have any excuse. You do know, and you *will not believe.*"

If the Jews were still in the condition where they had no evidence, then God would not judge them as he now judges them, on the basis of what Christ did. The Jews would not believe the evidence of their own eyes. They hated Jesus without a just cause. They hated him, and thus they hated the Father.

This very evidence of which Jesus speaks now makes us all accountable to God. We have read the eye-witness testimony, we have heard the words of Jesus, and now we will be judged according to our actions, even as the Jews were judged. We no longer have any excuse for sin. Jesus came into the world to declare the truth of the gospel, to demonstrate the power of God, and to fulfill God's eternal plan.

We will be judged according to our actions.

Something to Think About

When we receive *knowledge* of who Jesus is, we receive *responsibility*.

> *Crown Him the Lord of life,*
> *Who triumphed o'er the grave,*
> *And rose victorious to the strife*
> *For those He came to save;*
> *His glories now we sing*
> *Who died, and rose on high,*
> *Who died eternal life to bring,*
> *And lives that death may die.*
> —"Crown Him with Many Crowns"

Something to Do

We have a responsibility to act upon the truth as taught by Jesus Christ. Prayerfully consider Jesus' words in John 5.

66

The Counselor

"But the Counselor, the Holy Spirit, whom the Father will send in my name, will teach you all things and will remind you of everything I have said to you."
—John 14:26

In the charismatic movement today, much emphasis is placed on the *person* of the Holy Spirit, and so very little emphasis is placed on what the coming of the Spirit meant. The coming of the Spirit meant the glorification of Christ. The coming of the Spirit meant the exaltation of the Lord Jesus.

The Holy Spirit doesn't seek exaltation for himself. He doesn't seek glory for himself. The Holy Spirit seeks the glory of Christ and he bears witness to Christ. So when you see people putting an inordinate emphasis on the ministry of the Holy Spirit, at the expense of the person of the Master, then you realize they have lost sight of the biblical commandment. The Bible teaches that the Holy Spirit will *testify* about Jesus.

In the charismatic and Pentecostal worlds we study the gifts of the Holy Spirit, we study the fruits of the Holy Spirit, we discuss the power of the Holy Spirit, but we rarely get into Christ's intimate dialogues on the *meaning* of the Spirit's presence in our lives. It means something absolutely incredible.

I think one of the great weaknesses of the Charismatic movement is found right here in verse 26. They talk about the Holy Spirit—the gifts, the fruits, and the ministry—constantly singing hymns and praises to the work the Spirit does, but the primary work of the Spirit in the life of the believer is not any of these things. *The primary work of the Holy Spirit is to teach you to be more like Christ.* The Holy Spirit hasn't come to the Church to focus our attention on himself; he has come to the Church to focus our attention on Christ. The practical outgrowth of the Spirit's presence is teach,

> **The primary work of the Holy Spirit is to teach you to be more like Christ.**

teach, teach—which means learn, learn, learn.

And that is the weakness—that we who speak so much about the reality, and ministry, and power of the Spirit are so unwilling to submit to him when he teaches us. Instead, we submit to evangelists; we submit to our favorite Bible teachers and television personalities; we submit to whoever attracts us, rather than recognizing that everyone who attracts us is to be tested by the Word of God—measured by fidelity to the Holy Spirit. The Holy Spirit is supposed to protect us from twisted doctrine and television con artists.

Now you may say, "Well, why doesn't he protect us?" *Because you won't listen!* The Spirit speaks through the Scriptures, and if you're not going to stick your nose in the Scriptures, you're not going to get it by osmosis, praying in tongues, or someone laying hands on you. You will get it by opening your mind, using your vocabulary, and studying to show yourself approved by God. The people who study, listen, and learn are the people who grow. That's what God wants. That's the ministry of the Holy Spirit: to teach you all things.

Jesus wants us to get our priorities straight and to understand the true ministry of the Spirit. The ministry of the Holy Spirit is to *exalt Jesus,* to dispense fruit and gifts to us, and to bring us to spiritual maturity.

―○〇○―

Something to Think About

The Holy Spirit seeks the glory of Christ.

> *Thou art the bread of life,*
> *O Lord, to me,*
> *Thy holy Word the truth*
> *That saveth me;*
> *Give me to eat and live*
> *With thee above;*

Teach me to love thy truth,
For thou art love.

—"Break Thou the Bread of Life"

Something to Do

Study Psalm 1:1–6. Kneel in prayer and submit your heart to the teaching of the Holy Spirit. *Learn.*

67

The Windows of Heaven

I consider that our present sufferings are not worth comparing with the glory that will be revealed in us.
—Romans 8:18

Christians should take heart in the midst of persecution. They should say, "I'm *blessed* by God, because I wouldn't be getting this flack unless God was blessing me."

Sometimes at Christian Research Institute when we have problems, and believe me I think we have legions of demons assigned to us, it never fails but we get blessed out of our socks. It's an unfailing truth—something happens. God does something *incredible* and pours out a blessing, and you simply can't believe what happened.

Let me illustrate: December is the worst month of the year for Christian giving. CRI takes a terrible beating in December along with other Christian organizations, mainly because everyone's out buying Christmas presents. There's nothing wrong with that, but the devil is still in business in December. The work of God still has to go on in December. Just because people are trimming their trees doesn't mean the devil isn't trying to trim us!

Every December we have a special prayer session at CRI. One year we prayed asking, "Lord, this year we've had such a tough time from so many different sources. The devil's been after us in every area. We've got the building now, and all the problems that come with it. Lord, bless us out of our socks in December so that we'll know you're pleased with us during the year and that you'll bless us next year. We lay a fleece before you, Lord. Do something unusual. Every December is a bummer, but this time, please, just bless us. Open the windows of heaven and let us feel your power."

That December we got more money than we'd ever gotten in any December in the history of Christian Research Institute. It even beat out May, which is the best month of the year. God answered that fleece. It was as if he put his arm around our shoulders and gave us a nice squeeze. I could almost hear him saying, "OK! December's your worst month? I'm going to make it your greatest!" And he did. We just praised and thanked God for such a blessing; a blessing made greater by the fact that we closed for ten days during December for vacation, and "The Bible Answer Man" was not recorded live for most of the month. God blessed us more than we ever anticipated.

Jesus is trying to get the same message across to you—not just in finances—but in every area of your life. He wants you to realize how blessed you are when men persecute you. Don't rob yourself of a blessing by sticking your head under the covers saying, "It's a rainy day, and I'm not coming out." Instead, throw off the covers, bound out of bed, and ask God to do something unusual for you. God will not fail.

_____
God will not fail.

―ᘒ ᘒ―

Something to Think About

God will open the windows of heaven for *you.*

> *Perfect submission, all is at rest,*
> *I in my Savior am happy and blest:*
> *Watching and waiting, looking above,*
> *Filled with His goodness, lost in His love.*
>
> *This is my story, this is my song,*
> *Praising my Savior all the day long;*
> *This is my story, this is my song,*
> *Praising my Savior all the day long.*
>
> —"Blessed Assurance"

―ᘒ ᘒ―

Something to Do

Matthew 5:11–12 teaches us this: "Blessed are you when people insult you, persecute you and falsely say all kinds of evil against you because of me. Rejoice and be glad, because great is your reward in heaven." Remember to take heart in the midst of persecution. Ask God to do something *unusual* for you.

68

You Can't Outgive God

I have fought the good fight, I have finished the race,
I have kept the faith. Now there is in store for me the
crown of righteousness, which the Lord, the righteous
Judge, will award to me on that day.
                                                    —2 Timothy 4:7–8

January 1, 1989
Newport Mesa Christian Center Sunday Bible Class
Question and Answer Period

CLASS MEMBER: Good morning, Walter! We are praying for you.
Please keep up the good work! What are your concerns for 1989—
spiritually, financially, and worldwide?

WALTER MARTIN: Good morning! Well, I'd like to make it
through the year and be here next year in 1990 to keep on doing what
I'm doing! That's one of my major concerns.

Spiritually, I want to win as many souls as I possibly can and teach
the Church how to stay away from as much error as possible.
Financially, I have no complaints. The Lord has been gracious to me
and provided for my every need. I'm not rolling in dough, but God
has provided for me and for my family, and I'm grateful for that.
That's why monies which are given to me go to Christian Research
Institute. People all over the place give me money, and they say, "This
is for you." I'm very grateful for people giving me personal gifts and

I thank them for their consideration and their kindness, but to profit from the ministry in that respect, I would find difficult to do. And so I believe in turning all this in to Christian Research Institute.

Why? Because *you can't outgive God.* I give as much as I can, and do you know something? The more I give, the more blessings there are! Not just financially, but *blessings.*

My wife Darlene and I once had a serious disagreement about how to spend money for God. And *she who must be obeyed* told me that I should have more consideration for the budget than I did. It had to do with a royalty check I had received. I had decided I would give this money to a specific work for the Lord. My wife became a little upset and said, "We *need* that money!" And I answered, "You're right, but I see in my spirit that it's needed elsewhere, and I'm going to do this."

Well, we had a disagreement. We don't have arguments; we have in-depth discussions. And, since my wife is subject to her husband as the Church is subject to Christ, she finally conceded, "You do what you want to do; it's your money." That was the closing caveat. I said, "No, it's God's money. Let's do with it what God wants." So, I did it.

I think it was the next day, another check came from one of my publishers for a little bit more than what I had given the day before. My wife opened the envelope and looked at the check. When she saw the amount, she said, "Never again."

"What do you mean?" I asked.

"I will never question you again. You give anything you want, wherever you want to give it. The Lord will provide." And he has.

> *Never give to God to get something from God; you'll get a sore spiritual behind.*

We have a financial obligation to give whatever resources we have into the hands of the Lord. God blesses that. Never give to God to get something from God; you'll get a sore spiritual behind. He will not put up with that nonsense. But when you give, give expecting nothing. Give in trust and in love, and I *guarantee* you—after forty-four years of experience as a Christian—Jehovah will provide.

My worldwide concerns are that the gospel will go out every place it hasn't been before; and that Christians will *defend* their faith as well as proclaim their faith.

(*Author's Note:* Dad went home to be with the Lord, June 26, 1989.)

—ᘓ ᘔ—

Something to Think About

Face to face—Oh blissful moment!
Face to face—to see and know;
Face to face with my Redeemer,
Jesus Christ who loves me so.

Face to face I shall behold Him,
Far beyond the starry sky;
Face to face, in all His glory,
I shall see Him by and by!
   —"Face to Face with Christ, My Savior"

—ᘓ ᘔ—

Something to Do

Write down your concerns—spiritually, financially, and worldwide. Pray.

69

The Heart of Christianity

> Who is the liar? It is the man who denies that Jesus
> is the Christ. Such a man is the antichrist—he denies
> the Father and the Son. No one who denies the Son
> has the Father; whoever acknowledges the Son has
> the Father also.
>
> —1 John 2:22–23

What is a primary doctrine of the demons? The denial that Jesus
Christ is really God in human flesh. This is the denial of the occultic
and the cultic world across the board, so to speak. John says that whoever denies Jesus is Christ is the antichrist. Whoever denies that Jesus
Christ has come in the flesh is not of God. The cults deny Jesus is the
Christ by saying he has not come in the flesh. They teach this: He has
not come as *incarnation*. They attack the heart of Christianity—incar-
national theology. They'll call Jesus *anything* but Lord.

The core of Christianity is that Jesus is Lord, to the glory of God the
Father. Every tongue shall confess it one day. God became man.
Whoever denies that God became man teaches the doctrine of the
demons. This is the primary target of Satan: He must undercut the person of the Master. He dare not have the worship of the Lord Jesus
because he seeks worship for himself.
Remember his words to Christ in Matthew 4:9,
"'All this I will give you,' he said, 'if you will
bow down and worship me.'"

---
*Jesus is Lord, to the
glory of God the
Father.*

—⌐⌐ ⌐⌐—

Something to Think About

Whoever denies that God became man teaches the doctrine of the demons.

> *I stand amazed in the presence*
> *Of Jesus the Nazarene,*
> *And wonder how He could love me,*
> *A sinner, condemned unclean.*
>
> *How marvelous! how wonderful!*
> *And my song shall ever be;*
> *How marvelous! how wonderful*
> *Is my Savior's love for me!*
>   —"I Stand Amazed in the Presence"

—⌐⌐ ⌐⌐—

Something to Do

Make time to worship God today. Study the enemy's strategy. Remember the five planks in the doctrine of the demons:

1. Jesus as *a* way, not *the* way.
2. Get people absorbed with the future.
3. Get people to play with what they have no power over.
4. Equate the truth with mythology.
5. Deny that Jesus Christ is God in human flesh.

70

_⸙ ⸙_

Are You Transformed?

And we, who with unveiled faces all reflect the Lord's glory, are being transformed into his likeness with ever-increasing glory, which comes from the Lord, who is the Spirit.

—2 Corinthians 3:18

What does it mean to live in Christ so far as the world is concerned? We know as Christians that to live the Christian life is to allow the Spirit of God to work out his fruit and his gifts in our lives. We know that we must put to death on a regular basis the things that pervert our witness, change our values, and would lead us back into the old paths of sin. Every Christian knows that.

We are also told by Paul, in his Epistle to the Colossians, that we should seek the things from above. In Romans he warned us not to be *conformed* to the world in which we find ourselves, but to be *transformed* by the renewing of our minds. So there is a spiritual change, a change of focus, and a change of mind. The spiritual change means I have died in Christ, been buried with him in baptism, and raised with him in the newness of life. Now I focus on the things from above, where Christ dwells at the right hand of God. This does not mean you spend your time being so busy in spiritual pursuits that you forget the world in which you live. People who are homeless, cold, and starving must be cared for. The change of mind comes when we recognize the fact that our lives have to undergo change. The question is not "Are you born again?" The question is, *"Are you transformed?"* Do you think the things of God naturally or do you have to work at it? Does the fruit of the Holy Spirit grow out of your life naturally or are you striving, as a woman in labor, to produce fruit? That is not how fruit is produced. Fruit grows out of your life. It is produced *naturally*.

If you are bearing fruit, you are in God's will; you are doing what he wants you to do. If you are bearing fruit in Christ, you have every right to ask what you will of him and if you are in accordance with his will, *he hears you*.

If you are in the will of God you won't be asking for outlandish things, you won't be trying to get stuff for yourself, you won't be on what I call the "gimmee trip"—always asking God to give you something. Instead, you can be asking God for more power to understand his Word, for more grace to reach out to the lives of other people, and for more opportunities to bear witness for him. And you can be thanking and praising him for all the benefits and blessings he has already given.

We seek the things from above for the purpose of caring about the things that are below. When we become dead to sin and alive in Christ, we should think the thoughts of God. To rise with Christ is to live in the newness of a transformed life, and the power to do that comes from the Holy Spirit and the Word of God. The focus of our lives is resurrection and service; to walk with him and to fulfill the righteousness of God, which is by faith, in our daily walk.

The focus of our lives is resurrection and service.

Something to Think About

We must put to death on a regular basis the things that pervert our witness, change our values, and that would lead us back into the old paths of sin.

> *O Master, let me walk with Thee*
> *In lowly paths of service free;*
> *Tell me Thy secret, help me bear*
> *The strain of toil, the fret of care.*
> —"O Master, Let Me Walk With Thee"

Something to Do

John 15:1–17 teaches God's expectations and offers his promises. Write down what God expects of you and what He promises to give you if you obey.

71

_⟿ ⟾_

Set Apart

Beyond all question, the mystery of godliness is great:
He appeared in a body, was vindicated by the Spirit,
was seen by angels, was preached among the nations,
was believed on in the world, was taken up in glory.
                                                    —1 Timothy 3:16

A mystery is connected with godliness in the Christian life. The word *mystery* does not mean something which *cannot* be understood.

> **Great is the mystery of godliness.**

Mystery in Greek means something which has not as yet been fully revealed. Great is the mystery of godliness. That means we don't have all the truth about it, but what we do know is enough to push us to seek for more. We need more from God in our lives. You can't get more of God, but you can get more *from* God.

The Scripture tells you that when God chose to enter the world, he entered it in a father/son relationship. When he chose to reveal himself fully at the end of the ages as he tells us, he revealed himself in his Son. This is part of the great mystery of godliness—that God gave his Son, Jesus Christ, so that we could be transformed to be more like him. God's will is not only that we don't perish, but that, through Jesus, we be set apart, transformed and eventually, honored. *Holiness, godliness,* and *sanctification* are words describing essentially the same thing: We are to be set apart. We are God's children.

Great is the mystery of *godlikeness*—to be *like* God. That does not mean to *be* God; that does not mean to be *a* god. It means to be *like* *him*. Mortals will put on immortality. Corruption will put on incorruption. Death will be swallowed up by life. We shall be like him.

What is the destiny of the Church? The throne of God! We are to sit with him—and that is the ultimate in supreme honor.

―⟨⟩⟨⟩―

Something to Think About

What does it mean to be "set apart"?

> *Sing the wondrous love of Jesus,*
> *Sing His mercy and His grace:*
> *In the mansions bright and blessed,*
> *He'll prepare for us a place.*
>
> *When we all get to heaven,*
> *What a day of rejoicing that will be!*
> *When we all see Jesus,*
> *We'll sing and shout the victory.*
> ―"When We All Get to Heaven"

―⟨⟩⟨⟩―

Something to Do

Reflect on Ephesians 4:17–32. "Be imitators of God, therefore, as dearly loved children" (Eph. 5:1).

72

It's Not the Money

Then he said to them, "Watch out! Be on your guard against all kinds of greed; a man's life does not consist in the abundance of his possessions."

"No servant can serve two masters. Either he will hate the one and love the other, or he will be devoted to the one and despise the other. You cannot serve both God and Money."

—Luke 12:15; 16:13

Gain is godliness? Profit is godliness? This is what we hear all the time from the faith teachers; this is what we hear all the time from the positive confession and prosperity doctrine. If you've got it, it must mean you're godly. If you have profit, prosperity, and possessions, then you are obviously living the Christian life and you are a triumphant, godly Christian. Mother Teresa wasn't godly; David Livingstone wasn't; William Carey couldn't be, and George Mueller never was—because they didn't have anything! They didn't own a sixteen-cylinder horse and buggy. No Cadillacs were parked in the driveway.

If God wanted everyone to be rich, we would have a disaster in the Church of unparalleled proportions. A great many people know in their hearts, just as I know, that they couldn't handle millions of dollars. They couldn't handle all kinds of money, because money is a corrupting influence, unless we're under the control of the Holy Spirit. It is unfortunate that money seems to get control of us, rather than us controlling it.

God wants to meet our needs. He promised that. I believe God wants you to be happy as a witness for him and to enjoy the life we have here. But God also knows that we are sinners and sin corrupts and alters our lifestyle. God knows this, and that is why we need to go to the cross for forgiveness, and we have to *keep* going to Christ to be cleansed so we can serve him.

How many times have you heard people say, "Well, it's not the *money* I really care about; it's what the money can purchase. Money is nothing to me." Jesus answered that quite nicely in Matthew 6:21, "For where your treasure is, there your heart will be also." If it's in your new boat, your retirement fund, or your Mercedes, then Jesus says *that* is where your soul is. What a cold, dreary home for the soul—the abundance of our possessions!

> *What a cold, dreary home for the soul— the abundance of our possessions!*

---⌒ ⌒---

Something to Think About

Has your lifestyle been corrupted?

> *O the unsearchable riches of Christ!*
> *Who shall their greatness declare!*
> *Jewels whose luster our lives may adorn,*
> *Pearls that the poorest may wear!*
>
> *Precious, more precious—*
> *Wealth that can never be told;*
> *O the unsearchable riches of Christ—*
> *Precious, more precious than gold!*
> —"Unsearchable Riches"

---⌒ ⌒---

Something to Do

> "He chose David his servant
>   and took him from the sheep pens;
> from tending the sheep he brought him
>   to be the shepherd of his people Jacob,
>   of Israel his inheritance.
> And David shepherded them with integrity of heart;
>   with skillful hands he led them."
> —Psalm 78:70–72

Examine your heart.

73

God's Grace

I have been crucified with Christ and I no longer live,
but Christ lives in me. The life I live in the body, I live
by faith in the Son of God, who loved me and gave
himself for me.

—Galatians 2:20

Parents should appreciate this verse tremendously. Scripture teaches us here that we have an opportunity to be the priest before God and the representation of holiness to our children. We have the chance to manifest the purity of God in spiritual leadership. We have the great opportunity to be *like God* to our children, so they can see Christ in us, the hope of glory.

How do you get this in your life? The apostle Paul tells us in these two simple sentences. You have been cruci-

> *Christ will live the life of God in you when you permit him to do so.*

fied in Christ and Christ is alive in you. Christ will live the life of God in you when you permit him to do so. You must look at the character of Christ, which is the image of God. Look at the Son. Look at his righteousness. Look at his holiness. Look at his mercy. Then ask God for his grace.

You can't attain holiness by your efforts, by your works, or by your striving. You can't attain it through your desire or through gallons of tears shed in repentance. Holiness is *bestowed* by the grace of God. It works out in our lives through the grace of the Lord Jesus Christ.

Something to Think About

We have the great opportunity to be *like God* to our children, so they can see Christ in us, the hope of glory.

> *Take time to be holy,*
> *The world rushes on;*
> *Spend time in secret*
> *With Jesus alone:*
> *By looking to Jesus,*
> *Like Him thou shalt be;*
> *Thy friends in thy conduct*
> *His likeness shall see.*
> —"Take Time to Be Holy"

Something to Do

The word *holy* means pure and consecrated. Look to Jesus and take time to be holy.

74

The Hand of Jesus

"I have given them the glory that you gave me, that they may be one as we are one: I in them and you in me. May they be brought to complete unity to let the world know that you sent me and have loved them even as you have loved me."

—John 17:22–23

Jesus told us that when we pray, we should pray this way, "Our Father in heaven . . ." (Matt. 6:9). In other words, our relationship with God is the *intimate* relationship of child and parent. When you see a child take Mommy or Daddy's hand, and walk with security amidst other people or anything that might threaten them, you know the child is being protected by the parent. You may have children and have done it yourself.

What you don't realize most of the time as a Christian—and sometimes I don't stop to think about it either—is that in Jesus Christ, *God has given us his hand.* He walks with us through the world, through our tribulations, through our trials, through the attacks of Satan—he's there. The hand never lets go. You may sometimes try and wiggle out of it, but your security rests in the hand that holds you. That's the intimacy of parent and child.

Jesus said, "My father and I are intimately involved in an eternal relationship—and you are now involved in our relationship too."

182

In this chapter of John, Christ talks about intimacy between the Father, the Son, and the Church. Jesus said, "My father and I are intimately involved in an eternal relationship—and you are now involved in our relationship too." He prays that we be in union with him and with the Father, the same way he is in union with his Father. This is a revelation! We are in union with God in a way that has never been known before; we have an intimacy with him that has never been disclosed before.

You and I can't ever be gods because there is only one God. We can't be God, because God alone is eternal and we're finite. So what God is trying to tell us here is he has *adopted* us into his family and bestowed upon us his family name. We are not deity, but we are his children and we inherit as his children exactly what his Son inherits.

In Jesus Christ, we are the heirs of the glory of God. That may come as quite a jolt to our rather stunted minds, at least it always has to mine. But, nevertheless, it's true. It is so wonderful, so incomprehensible that its truthfulness sometimes slips by us. It shouldn't. When God says we will inherit and sit with him in his throne, by "throne" he means the center of authority, the center of power, the center of glory. The very center of heaven itself is the throne of God. Now, angels sing his praises *around* his throne, but the Church inherits to *sit with him in his throne*. That stunning fact escapes us most of the time.

You may ask, "Do you mean that some day I am going to sit at the center of authority—all power, all knowledge, all wisdom? That I will sit in the midst of the Shekinah of Yahweh Elohim, which destroys anything that looks at it? I'm going to be there in an immortal body?" Yes! And not only are you going to be there in an immortal body, but you're going to judge the angels! I can't wait until Lucifer comes before me—I'm going to get my licks in then!

You see, we don't understand! We don't understand that we have been *destined* for the throne of God; that we have been predestined to share in his glory. The glory that Christ and God had before time has been given to the Church when we enter his presence. We are not gods. We are not goddesses. We are not deity. We are *redeemed* children of our Father, and as his children we are heirs and joint heirs with Christ.

—⟨∘ ∘⟩—

Something to Think About

Our relationship with God is the *intimate* relationship of child and parent. *God has given us his hand.*

His forever, only His;
Who the Lord and me shall part?
Ah, with what a rest of bliss
Christ can fill the loving heart!
Heaven and earth may fade and flee,
Firstborn light in gloom decline;
But while God and I shall be,
I am His and He is mine.
      —"I Am His and He Is Mine"

Something to Do

God's hand never lets go! You may sometimes try to wiggle out of it, but your security rests in the hand that holds you. Trust in that security.

75

Tell the Truth

Dear children, this is the last hour; and as you have heard that the antichrist is coming, even now many antichrists have come.

—1 John 2:18

We are now accelerating toward the consummation of time. The restoration of Israel, the conglomeration of world powers, the atmosphere of general unbelief and antagonism to the Christian gospel— all confirm this truth. When *Time* magazine can describe this as the "post-Christian" era; when we see the rise of the cults, false prophets, and false teachers who speak to us using the name of Jesus but deny the identity and power of Jesus Christ, then we know that we are arriving rapidly at the consummation of time.

One of the prevailing attitudes we face today is "Don't say *anything* about the cults. Whatever you do, don't say anything about them!" Why is this attitude so prevalent? Because people are afraid that if you tell what's really going to happen to those who reject the Lord Jesus; if you alienate them, they won't listen to the gospel.

> We have turned away from the challenge of the first century: The early Christians turned the world upside down because they dared to confront evil.

This is a very dangerous philosophy. It is a non-Christian philosophy. Today an enormous amount of people are involved in the cults and the occult, and the Church is not penetrating them with a major witness.

Why? *We have turned away from the challenge of the first century:* The early Christians turned the world upside down because they dared to confront evil. The rise of the cults is evil. It uses the vocabulary of Christianity. It uses the name of Jesus, but it has another Jesus, another spirit, and a foreign gospel. Jesus wanted to impress upon the Church that there is such a thing as deception, and that we will be inundated by it at the end of the ages. We must do as the early Church did, and dare to confront evil.

When I talk about things like this, people sometimes get very irritated. They say, "Why are you attacking other people's religions?" I'm not! As a minister of the gospel of Jesus Christ and as a professor of comparative religions, I have to *respond* to the attacks made upon Christianity. Otherwise, I am not faithful to my ordination vows and I am not faithful to the preaching of the cross. It is necessary to accept the risk of being hated, despised, rejected, and persecuted by the very people that you are trying to evangelize—and you can get into this position simply by telling people the truth.

One of today's great errors is the idea that it's unloving to tell people the truth. If you tell a Jehovah's Witness he's going to hell without the real Jesus, the Jehovah's Witness gets mad. You didn't expect him to pin any Sunday school medals on you, did you? You didn't expect the devil to recommend you for the Heavenly Congressional Medal of Honor, did you? Of course not—*we are at war* with the forces of darkness. Scripture says to, "Put on the full armor of God" (Eph. 6:11). Why do you put on armor if you're not in a war?

The most loving being that ever walked this earth was the Son of God. Jesus Christ was love incarnate. I want you to listen to love in human flesh when he met the cults and the false teachers of his day: "Woe to you, teachers of the law and Pharisees, you hypocrites! You are like whitewashed tombs, which look beautiful on the outside but on the inside are full of dead men's bones and everything unclean" (Matt. 23:27). "You snakes! You brood of vipers! How will you escape being condemned to hell?" (Matt. 23:33). *That* is incarnate love.

All Christians must wake up to the fact that we are born in conflict. We are not to keep quiet in the presence of evil. We have arrived in the times where men will not put up with sound teaching. We're here! They will accept *anything* but the gospel, because the gospel demands the submission of the total human being to the redemption of God. The gospel demands that you see yourself as you really are—

a lost sinner, desperately in need of a Savior. It is the responsibility of the Church to hold that message out.

— ᴄᴏ ᴏᴏ —

Something to Think About

We must do as the early Church did and dare to confront evil.

> *Sweetly echo the gospel call,*
> *Wonderful words of life;*
> *Offer pardon and peace to all,*
> *Wonderful words of life;*
>
> *Jesus, only Savior,*
> *Sanctify forever,*
> *Beautiful words, wonderful words,*
> *Wonderful words of life.*
> —"Wonderful Words of Life"

— ᴄᴏ ᴏᴏ —

Something to Do

Don't keep quiet in the presence of evil. Hold the message out.

76

It's His Kingdom

Is any one of you sick? He should call the elders of the church to pray over him and anoint him with oil in the name of the Lord.

—James 5:14

Do you know why some people won't pray for the sick? *They're embarrassed.* They're scared to death if they lay hands on someone who's sick and the person isn't healed, it's going to reflect on them.

I once had a dear friend who was a Jewish convert to Christianity. He had a great sense of humor, and we'd spend time together laughing and talking about many different issues. One afternoon, we were discussing the difficult subject of praying for the sick. He interrupted me in the middle of a sentence, put his hand on my shoulder and said, "So it shouldn't be a total loss, I'll give you some advice."

"Give me the advice," I said.

"Pray for the sick, no matter what they look like or how impossible it is—no matter what the circumstances. Don't be embarrassed. Pray for them. It's God's kingdom; *he should worry.*"

God touches people and miraculously restores them for his purpose and his glory.

I never forgot that. Why should I be embarrassed? God said to pray for them and anoint them with oil, right? God said to do it—fine, I'll do it. If God doesn't heal them, it's his worry—it's his kingdom. All I'm doing is what he told me to do. What is there to be embarrassed about? I pray for everybody, and

188

when he wants to, God touches people and miraculously restores them for his purpose and his glory.

___ ❧ ❧ ___

Something to Think About

"Summon your power, O God; show us your strength, O God, as you have done before" (Ps. 68:28).

> *Out of my bondage, sorrow and night,*
> *Jesus, I come, Jesus, I come;*
> *Into Thy freedom, gladness and light,*
> *Jesus, I come to Thee;*
> *Out of my sickness into Thy health,*
> *Out of my want and into Thy wealth,*
> *Out of my sin and into Thyself,*
> *Jesus, I come to Thee.*
> —"Out of My Bondage, Sorrow, and Night"

___ ❧ ❧ ___

Something to Do

Pray for the sick, no matter what they look like or how impossible it seems.

77

_ᕋ ᕌ_

Jesus Christ Is Unique

For if the dead are not raised, then Christ has not been raised either. And if Christ has not been raised, your faith is futile; you are still in your sins.
—1 Corinthians 15:16–17

The resurrection of Christ is not just an Easter time phenomenon to be celebrated in song and service, but the Resurrection is literally the dawn of every new day of our lives and of our witness—because he lives, we will live also (John 11:25).

It is obvious that the concept of resurrection is inherent in the very structure of New Testament theology. The early Christians were absorbed or *obsessed*, if we use the word correctly, with the concept of resurrection. The synoptic Gospels of Matthew, Mark, and Luke all mention the resurrection of the Lord Jesus Christ. John wrote about it in great detail in the twentieth chapter, specifically spelling out that "these are written that you may believe that Jesus is the Christ, the Son of God, and that by believing you may have life in his name" (John 20:31). Believing *what?* Believing he is the Son of God *with power by resurrection* from among the corpses. In other words, if Christ is not raised from among the corpses, how then is he the Son of God? He couldn't save himself!

Jesus Christ is unique. He is the firstborn from among the dead.

Jesus Christ is unique. He is the firstborn from among the dead. By man came death, and by man came also the resurrection from the dead. The apostle Paul put this into perspective when he wrote in Acts 26 that we should not think it an incredible thing that God resurrects the dead. When one is dealing with an all powerful being—the God of the galaxies—one should have no problem understanding that he can wield sufficient energy not only to resurrect all the corpses of earth, but also to recreate a billion earths in any stage of development he chooses, simply by command. The Scripture says he commands the things that are not, as if they were. He calls them into existence by his laws, sustains them, and when he finishes with them, annihilates them. Why? Because all power is his in heaven and in earth.

You and I cannot even begin to conceive of such power. We explore the thermonuclear weapon and we think it fantastic. How this must amuse the infinite intellect that belongs to Almighty God, when he looks at us floating around on a semiburned-out cinder in our little solar system, ninety-three million miles from a nuclear furnace; a furnace which could explode at any moment and exudes more energy in a few seconds than all the atomic bombs and hydrogen bombs we have exploded up to the present moment. This rather diminishes *our concept* of power.

The fact we are discussing here is the *enormity* of the God who *is,* and who has the power to raise from the dead. In the light of this concept of the God of creation, is it an incredible thing that God raises the dead? It is only incredible for nitwits who cannot perceive that an infinite being can do whatever he wants to do.

The whole record of the New Testament, the whole record of truth, is that *God raised Jesus Christ from among the corpses.* He is alive today, and because he lives we will live also. The resurrection of Christ is not just an Easter celebration. It is the hope that should fill us with joy every day of our lives.

—◦ ◦—

Something to Think About

Each new day of your life and of your witness you have because *he lives.*

> *I sing the mighty power of God*
> *That made the mountains rise,*
> *That spread the flowing seas abroad*
> *And built the lofty skies.*
> *I sing the wisdom that ordained*

The sun to rule the day;
The moon shines full at His command,
And all the stars obey.
　　　—"I Sing the Mighty Power of God"

Something to Do

Study Ephesians 1:15–23. Meditate on the power of God.

78

The Sin-Bearer

For since the creation of the world God's invisible qualities—his eternal power and divine nature— have been clearly seen, being understood from what has been made, so that men are without excuse.

—Romans 1:20

God doesn't send people to hell because they haven't heard the name of Jesus. We have no way of knowing how God communicates with people. Surely, the gospel went out from Jerusalem and Judea to the uttermost parts of the earth. God obviously had to consider the fact that there were no jet airplanes, no modern means of transportation, and that people on the other side of the earth could hardly be charged in the same category with people who were right there in Jerusalem. So he must have had a plan for dealing with them. The Judge of the whole earth will do what is right!

> The Judge of the whole earth will do what is right!

He sent us into the world to preach the gospel so that men might be saved; that does not mean God doesn't consider the fact that people—through no fault of their own—have not heard the gospel. I think *that* truth is very clearly taught in Romans 1, which then explains how God has revealed himself to them. Don't ask me how, because I don't know.

Dr. Frank Gaebelin once told me about a missionary who had gone to a part of the world where the gospel had never been preached. Dr. Gaebelin's story was very well-documented, and he talked personally with this man.

A certain missionary felt a compulsion to go to a specific part of Africa. When he arrived in the village and started preaching Christ, he was amazed by the response. Instead of the indifference or even outright hostility he expected to encounter, people were clearly astonished by his words and very happy to see him. They started talking with each other, buzzing like a huge beehive, and he asked them, "What is the problem? Have I done something wrong?"

"No," they answered. "But you're talking about the *Sin-bearer*."

"The Sin-bearer!" he repeated, amazed at this revelation. Yes, he agreed, Jesus was the Sin-bearer but *how did they know that?* One of the elders of the tribe smiled broadly at him, and told him there was someone he must meet. They led him to a small house on the outskirts of the village, where an elderly man waited to speak with him. The missionary would never forget this conversation. The old man told him he knew the world was created by an eternal, good being and that he had sought for him. He'd actually prayed for God to reveal himself to him, and the Lord had answered his prayer. God gave this man, this pagan back in darkest Africa, a vision of Christ on the cross! And he didn't understand anything except that there was a Sin-bearer and that the message would come to them.

The missionary told Dr. Gaebelin, "It was the easiest preaching I've ever done. They were waiting for me. I preached and practically the whole tribe got saved! The old man's face shone like a saint's."

I believe that man had a vision of Christ. God communicated with him and the gospel came to them as a result of that. There are enough instances of this in China and in other parts of the world to prove to me that *God cares* about these people.

I have to believe that the God of the Bible is just. If people go to hell, they go not because they haven't heard the name of Jesus, but because they *turn away* from the knowledge that God makes available to them. They could turn *toward him* instead of away. And if they do, he will send the gospel to them. I believe that is the truth. God is not going to arbitrarily send people off to hell if they turn—even *blink*— in his direction. He does not want any to perish (2 Pet. 3:9).

—◦ ◦—

Something to Think About

God reveals himself to people who search for him because *God cares about people.*

There's not a plant or flower below
But makes Thy glories known;
And clouds arise and tempests blow,
By order from Thy throne;
While all that borrows life from Thee
Is ever in Thy care,
And everywhere that man can be,
Thou, God, art present there.
— "I Sing the Mighty Power of God"

Something to Do

Pray that the gospel might reach those waiting to hear it.

79

_⌒ ⌒_

The Fickle Human Heart

While they were listening to this, he went on to tell them a parable, because he was near Jerusalem and the people thought that the kingdom of God was going to appear at once. He said: "A man of noble birth went to a distant country to have himself appointed king and then to return. So he called ten of his servants and gave them ten minas. 'Put this money to work,' he said, 'until I come back.'

"But his subjects hated him and sent a delegation after him to say, 'We don't want this man to be our king.'"

—Luke 19:11–14

Before his triumphal entry into Jerusalem, Jesus told the people a parable, and therefore this parable has enormous historical and chronological significance. In the first part of the story he talked about the coming of the kingdom. The people of that day *did not know the time* of their visitation. They thought the "kingdom" would come at once, and when it didn't, they turned away. When the *true* kingdom of God itself was offered to them, they did not understand and turned from it.

Jesus says this just before he enters Jerusalem—before all the "hosannas," before the people give him a tumultuous welcome. *He knows their hearts before they do.* These are the same people who, not long afterward,

How fickle, how fragile is the human heart and the emotion of the moment.

will be out there shouting, "Crucify him! Crucify him! We have no king but Caesar!" How fickle, how fragile is the human heart and the emotion of the moment. It changes like the current and the tide—suddenly—and in this case, for their own destruction.

Jesus points to himself as the king in this parable. He says, "Let me tell you something: This king is *me* and the citizens here are the Jews. They may yell 'hosanna' today, but they will end up saying, 'We will not have this man reign over us,' tomorrow." And that's exactly what they did. Jesus told this parable when he did for many reasons, one of which was this: He wanted us to know that *he knew* in advance what was going to happen. And even then, he tried to warn them. He tried to teach them but they would not listen. How well he knows the fickle human heart, and still, he loves us.

_⚬ ⚬_

Something to Think About

God knows your heart before you do.

> *Rock of ages, cleft for me,*
> *Let me hide myself in Thee;*
> *Let the water and the blood,*
> *From Thy wounded side which flowed,*
> *Be of sin the double cure,*
> *Save from wrath and make me pure.*

> *Could my tears forever flow,*
> *Could my zeal no weakness know,*
> *These for sin could not atone,*
> *Thou must save, and Thou alone:*
> *In my hand no price I bring,*
> *Simply to Thy cross I cling.*
> —"Rock of Ages, Cleft for Me"

_⚬ ⚬_

Something to Do

Read Luke 19:11–27.

80

The Fire of Judgment

*He was made king, however, and returned home.
Then he sent for the servants to whom he had given
the money, in order to find out what they had gained
with it.*

—Luke 19:15

At the end of this parable, Jesus judges those who *did* receive him and those who did serve him. Some responded and did what they were supposed to do. They were Jews and Gentiles who would be judged on the basis of what they did with what they were given. The money only illustrates one type of "investment" of what you have for God.

How did you invest what God gave you? Did God give you a good mind and you spent your time glued to a television set? *Unprofitable servant.* Did God give you resources and did you take those resources and plow them into the kingdom of heaven to the best of your ability? Or did you horde them? Unprofitable servant. Did you invest your talents in the life that you had—in your witness to your friends, neighbors, and church? Did you care for the sick? Did you feed the hungry at Easter and Christmas? Did you reach out to clothe those who didn't have anything? Did you care about what happened in Bangladesh or someplace else in the world? Did you think about investing *there* what God had given you? Or did you just keep yourself in your own little orbit, in your own little private life?

You see, Christ is telling you, "I gave you this. I gave you whatever you've got. But I didn't give it to you for you to consume it upon your desires. I gave it to you so that you might *invest* it in my kingdom. When you fed and clothed someone—when you showed the compassion of the Holy Spirit, it was as if *you were doing it for me*" (Matt. 25:31–46). That's what it means to invest. God isn't just addressing your bank account, he's talking about your life. Have you invested your time, your efforts, your resources, and the fruits of the Spirit God gave you? Or did you just put half of it in—or none of it? Jesus states that when he comes back, judgment begins at the house of the Lord. And if the righteous can scarcely be saved, how will the ungodly and the sinner make any appearance?

You see, this parable, anticipating his entry into Jerusalem, is to *warn* us, even as it warned the Jews who were not listening: There *is* a day of accountability. The time will come when God will turn to some and say, "You wicked and unprofitable servants." We're not talking about your salvation, now. We're talking about what you're going to lose, which is *everything* you thought valuable. All the rewards you thought were yours will be taken, and others will benefit from them.

> There is a day of accountability.

The foundation of Jesus Christ doesn't change, but the wood, the hay, and the stubble that you put on that foundation by *refusing to invest* your talents in the kingdom of God will be consumed on that day. All that will remain is the foundation. You will be saved, but the fire of God's judgment will consume everything else. This is a sobering, frightening warning, and it comes to those whom God has given something to invest.

Jesus knew well the fickle heart of man—some wanted nothing to do with him, others *everything.* The one he repudiated, the other he called his own. And he will judge his own according to the investment of the talents he's given him.

―◦ ◦―

Something to Think About

"The King will reply, 'I tell you the truth, whatever you did for one of the least of these brothers of mine, you did for me'" (Matt. 25:40).

I want to live above the world,
Though Satan's darts at me are hurled;
For faith has caught the joyful sound,
The song of saints on higher ground.

Lord, lift me up and let me stand,
By faith on heaven's tableland;
A higher plane than I have found;
Lord, plant my feet on higher ground.
         —"Higher Ground"

Something to Do

Invest your time, your efforts, your resources, and the fruits of the
Spirit God gave you.

81

Positive Thinking?

It is true that some preach Christ out of envy and
rivalry, but others out of good will. The latter do so in
love, knowing that I am put here for the defense of the
gospel. The former preach Christ out of selfish ambi-
tion, not sincerely.

—Philippians 1:15–17

The Scripture specifically indicates in numerous places that the
gospel must be defended. Paul was set for the "defense of the gospel."
Obviously, the implication is positive—it's not negative to defend the
gospel.

I'll never forget the time when my teacher, Donald Grey
Barnhouse, told me of a luncheon he had with Norman Vincent
Peale, who was then riding the crest of the wave on the power of pos-
itive thinking. They chatted for a few minutes when Dr. Peale said,
"I'd like a candid answer, Dr. Barnhouse. I know you'll give me one.
What do you really think of what I've written on the power of posi-
tive thought?"

Dr. Barnhouse was quiet for a moment, then replied, "Well, I can
only tell you what a great many clergy have said to me."

"And what is that?"

"Paul is appealing, but Peale is *appalling.*"

Dr. Peale choked on his soup—very upset by this—and exclaimed,
"What?"

"You have forgotten the most important thing," said Dr. Barnhouse, irrepressible as ever. "Before anyone can think positively, they must think *negatively.*"

"What do you mean by that?"

"Look," continued Barnhouse, "I am a sinner. Negative or positive?"

"Negative."

"I am a lost sinner. Negative or positive?"

"Negative."

"I am going to eternal judgement. Negative or positive?"

"Negative."

Barnhouse smiled, "Those are three negative propositions, without which you cannot think positively. 'Believe on the Lord Jesus Christ and thou shalt be saved' (Acts 16:31 KJV). But if you don't think the first three, you'll never get to the fourth."

"I never thought of it quite that way before," answered Dr. Peale, rather disturbed.

"You must write a new book," suggested Dr. Barnhouse—"*The Power of Negative Thinking.*"

"*I can't* do that; it would ruin me!"

"Get out the truth," said Barnhouse. "The Lord will take care of it."

Speak the truth in love, but for the sake of Christ, let's speak it!

He never wrote the book, but Dr. Peale was told what he should do. The truth of the matter is this: Whatever the cost, tell the truth. We must do this. Speak the truth in love, but for the sake of Christ, let's speak it!

People are looking for spiritual reality, spiritual truth. At this moment the gospel of Jesus Christ stands ready where no other power on earth is ready—because Jesus is ultimate reality.

─ ᔕ ᔐ ─

Something to Think About

Before anyone can think positively, they must think *negatively.*

> *Run the race*
> *thru God's good grace,*
> *Lift up your eyes,*
> *and seek his face;*
> *Life with its way*

before us lies,
Christ is the path
And Christ the prize.
　—"Fight the Good Fight"

Something to Do

"They exchanged the truth of God for a lie, and worshiped and served created things rather than the Creator—who is forever praised" (Rom. 1:25). Whatever the cost, tell the truth.

82

Is God Mad at Me?

What if some did not have faith? Will their lack of faith nullify God's faithfulness? Not at all!
—Romans 3:3–4

Jesus Christ heals today—but you don't run around laying hands on everyone claiming, "Jesus Christ heals you now," because you *don't know!* And If you do this, what devastation you wreak on people—*in* their lives. They start blaming themselves and going on guilt trips. They ask over and over again, "Why doesn't God heal me? There must be something wrong in my life. The Lord is mad at me!" Thy are wrecks.

I know this from experience. When I taught at Melodyland, I saw it over and over again. Every time one of the so-called "faith" teachers came through town, we got all the basket cases they left behind. It was not at all unusual to see one of these "teachers" stand in front of a line of people waiting for prayer, and after laying hands on them, if they were not visibly healed, the "teacher" responded, "You don't have enough faith." That's a *cruel* thing to say to a person who is suffering. How does he know someone's heart and how much faith they may or may not have? Who made him the Holy Spirit for the Church? How dare they take that upon themselves!

> *"Why doesn't God heal me? There must be something wrong in my life. The Lord is mad at me!"*

I applaud the idea of praying for the sick, and I do it myself. But the Scripture is very clear that *God decides* who is healed in accordance with *his* will—not yours! If we would leave it there, we wouldn't have the problems we have today with the "faith teachers," who are now into the Mind Science cults and the New Age Movement. They've crossed over from aberrant theology to heretical theology and cultic theology. That's dangerous! And that's why we have to speak out and say so!

Something to Think About

God decides who is healed in accordance with *his will*—not yours!

> *I heard the voice of Jesus say,*
> *"Come unto Me and rest;*
> *Lay down, thou weary one, lay down*
> *Thy head upon My breast."*
> *I came to Jesus as I was,*
> *Weary and worn and sad;*
> *I found in Him a resting place,*
> *And He has made me glad.*
> *—*"I Heard the Voice of Jesus Say"

Something to Do

Pray for those who are struggling daily with this issue of faith and healing. Ask for God's wisdom and peace in their lives.

83

_⊙ ⊙_

Inspiration

*Above all, you must understand that no prophecy of
Scripture came about by the prophet's own interpretation. For prophecy never had its origin in the will of
man, but men spoke from God as they were carried
along by the Holy Spirit.*

—2 Peter 1:20–21

Peter tells us here that no prophecy of God ever came by the will of
man. It didn't originate with someone sitting down and saying, "I
understand the culture, the geography, and the background. I understand the language and the context, and now I'm going to give a
prophecy consistent with that information." Never. It says that holy
men of God spoke "as they were carried along by the Holy Spirit." No
Scripture originates from an individual's point of view. It originates
with the Holy Spirit who breathes upon the person and literally car-
ries them along, so they might communicate the Word of God.

The basic principle of biblical inspiration is this: God breathed
through his Spirit upon the minds of men and their spirits and
caused them to record, without error, the
message that he wanted to communicate.
Simply speaking, that's called verbal inspiration. God gave it, and that verbal inspiration
extended to the entire text of Holy Scripture.

> *God breathed through
> his Spirit upon the
> minds of men and
> their spirits.*

Scripture was closed canonically in the first century of the Christian era. We know this because Jude 3 says, "once for all entrusted to the saints." So before the close of the first century, the faith of Christ—what was necessary for our salvation, the living of the Christian life, edification, and evangelism—already existed, *complete.*

We don't need Mary Baker Eddy. We don't need Charles and Myrtle Fillmore. We don't need Charles Russell and the Jehovah's Witnesses. We don't need the kingdom of the cults, and we don't need liberal theologians and destructive higher critics for you to arrive at the faith. The faith was "once for all entrusted to the saints."

Something to Think About

No Scripture originates from an individual's point of view. It originates with the Holy Spirit.

> *O send thy Spirit, Lord,*
> *Now unto me,*
> *That he may touch my eyes,*
> *And make me see:*
> *Show me the truth concealed*
> *Within thy Word,*
> *And in thy Book revealed*
> *I see thee, Lord.*
> —"Break Thou the Bread of Life"

Something to Do

Do you find it difficult to explain biblical inspiration? Review the definition and commit it to memory.

84

The Correct Tools

Do your best to present yourself to God as one approved, a workman who does not need to be ashamed and who correctly handles the word of truth.
—2 Timothy 2:15

The Christian is instructed, "Be thoroughly equipped for every good work" (2 Tim. 3:17). To do that you must *rightly interpret,* or correctly handle the Word of Truth. You must be carried along by the Holy Spirit in a manner consistent with Scripture. You must not deny Holy Scripture because of emotions or because of any subsequent material you may think is important. All materials are subject to what the Word of God specifically proclaims. They may be used to help you understand it, but they are not a *substitute* for it—nor can they judge Scripture. Scripture judges *all* forms of interpretation. Interpretational viewpoints do not govern Scripture.

> You must correctly handle the Word of Truth.

Christians have a basic hermeneutical or interpretational position: The Old Testament is *always* to be interpreted in the light of the New Testament—never the reverse. You may not build New Testament theology by quoting Old Testament passages without a link to the New Testament. This is, unfortunately, the root of a great deal of heresy.

The Bible is a book originating with God, and fully utilizing the vocabulary, the culture, the background, and the education of man.

So you must look at it as you would any other book in terms of language, geography, culture, and background. Once again, those things don't have the right to change Scripture, but they are valuable to give you a background in understanding Scripture. Secondly, if you're going to interpret, you should understand that biblical literature has prose, or poetry; it has history; it has allegory; it has literal and symbolic language—and you have to know *which is which*. Otherwise, you find yourself in an absolutely untenable position.

If you're going to interpret the Scripture, you should have some sense of historical background, so you don't approach a Bible book as if it was written *now*. You need to examine it in its historical context and in light of the culture that produced it. Then, you must understand the geographical conditions. You must understand the influence of terrain and climate, and how people viewed these things—what it meant to them. Next you need to understand the life setting: What kind of people do we meet in the Bible? You've got to get "under their skin." You have to look at the times through their eyes, not through yours.

You must remember that the Bible is an Eastern book—it is not Western nor Aristotelian. That's the way *we* think. The Bible is filled with paradoxes. It's filled with Eastern reasoning. That's why I always laugh when I'm debating people in transcendental meditation, Hindu-based cults, and Eastern religions, and they say to me, "Well, the problem with you is you're westernized. Christianity is a Western religion."

Oh, really? Jesus Christ was born in Asia. He lived in Asia. He worked his miracles in Asia. He was crucified in Asia. He rose from the dead in Asia, and he returns to Asia when his feet touch the Mt. of Olives. When Jesus comes back, where will he be? Not in Independence, Missouri, as the Mormons think, and not in Rome, as some Catholics think. When he returns his feet will touch the Mt. of Olives, and the mountain will split in two at his presence. Christianity is an Eastern religion.

These are the general principles of biblical interpretation, and every Christian should employ them. We are commanded to *rightly interpret* God's Word and to do that, you must use the correct tools.

―♻ ♻―

Something to Think About

Scripture judges *all* forms of interpretation. Interpretational viewpoints do not govern Scripture.

Thy Word is like a starry host—
A thousand rays of light
Are seen to guide the traveler,
And make his pathway bright.
O may I find my armor there,
Thy Word my trusty sword!
I'll learn to fight with every foe
The Battle of the Lord!
— "Thy Word Is Like a Garden, Lord,"

___◦◦___

Something to Do

Review, learn, and *use* the general principles of biblical interpretation.

85

Let's Talk about Jesus!

"O unbelieving and perverse generation," Jesus replied, "how long shall I stay with you? How long shall I put up with you?"

—Matthew 17:17

I once debated Madalyn Murray O'Hair, one of the foremost atheists in the world, for five hours on NBC. We got into a lengthy discussion during the debate on who Jesus was, and after she finished swearing (they had to edit about every fifth word she said), she finally got to the place where she wanted to say something directly against him. She seemed to be searching for the words to express it, but she couldn't come out on the air and tell me, because she knew the audience would never sit still for it. So, she kept dodging around the subject. She would say things like, "Well, the Bible has mistakes. The prophets made mistakes—and everybody knows this . . . and everybody knows that."

I said, "Madalyn, here's a Bible. Show me a few mistakes."

"I haven't got time for that," she snapped.

"Well, you're a lawyer, aren't you?"

"Yes."

"A good lawyer will *always* look at the evidence. I assume you're a good lawyer. Look at the evidence. Produce the mistakes!"

There was nothing she could produce. So I said to her, "Let's talk about Jesus!" We broke for a commercial just then and she was so angry, she almost *snarled* at me—like an animal.

211

When we went back on the air she couldn't snarl, so she began listing all the failures of Christianity. She kept going off into the history of the Church and circling around the person of Jesus Christ. Why? Because she had nothing she could say against him that could not be immediately refuted. It was easier for her to muddy up the waters than to fight me to prove her point.

Jesus Christ came into the world and stated, "I am the way and the truth and the life" (John 14:6). It's time the Church got up and answered the atheists, the agnostics, the skeptics, the cultists, and everyone else and said, "This is Christianity and that is of the *devil.*" Let's take a stand on it!

Let's take a stand on it!

_ᴄ⫶ ⫶ᴄ_

Something to Think About

It's easier for someone to muddy up the waters than to fight to prove a point.

Is your life a channel of blessing?
Is it daily telling for Him?
Have you spoken the word of salvation
To those who are dying in sin?

Make me a channel of blessing today,
Make me a channel of blessing, I pray;
My life possessing, my service blessing,
Make me a channel of blessing today.
    —"Make Me a Channel of Blessing"

_ᴄ⫶ ⫶ᴄ_

Something to Do

Don't allow someone to confuse the issue. Take them to the heart of the matter—Jesus Christ. There is nothing they can say about him that cannot be immediately refuted.

86

Let History Be the Judge

He who is pregnant with evil and conceives trouble gives birth to disillusionment. He who digs a hole and scoops it out falls into the pit he has made. The trouble he causes recoils on himself; his violence comes down on his own head.

—Psalm 7:14–16

I am so tired of critics pointing to all the so-called failures of Christianity throughout the ages. The truth is that Atheism and Agnosticism are responsible for more deaths than all the religious wars down through history!

In Germany, two men named Carl Marx and Frederick Ingles produced a philosophy called "Dialectical Materialism," which is known today as communism. In the fifty-odd years it has been in existence, that philosophy has destroyed—in real human lives—more than a hundred million people. In fifty years! Ten million Baptists *alone* died in Russia under Stalin, just because of that *"philosophy."*

"God is dead."—
Nietzsche
"Nietzsche is
dead."—God

Many philosophers say that Christianity is illogical and irrational. There used to be a saying in Germany when Frederic Nietzsche was alive: "God is dead." They wrote it all over the walls, because Nietzsche tried to prove that Christianity, Judaism, and the Bible were mythology.

When Nietzsche died, they changed the sign to: "Nietzsche is dead.—God." And that's exactly what happened: He departed the premises and God still remains. The philosophists succeed only in confusion and in refuting each other. They have been doing nothing but causing problems for almost two thousand years. Christianity is not illogical or irrational—the philosophers are.

You don't have to work yourself to death trying to refute philosophers—they refute each other! In the end, they all come back to the same thing: They don't know. They're all agnostic. That's why Paul tells you in Colossians to "beware." "See to it that no one takes you captive through hollow and deceptive philosophy, which depends on human tradition and the basic principles of this world rather than on Christ" (Col. 2:8).

The arrogant philosopher Nietzsche so influenced Adolph Hitler that he brought about the persecution of the Jews on the grounds they were an inferior race. Hitler believed the Germans were the Arian supermen of Nietzsche's philosophy. Six million Jews were eradicated on the basis of this line of reasoning. Communism and Nazism have managed, in the last fifty-odd years, to wipe out twenty times more people than Christianity is accused of in the last nineteen hundred years! Atheism is the great, beneficent helper of mankind? Let history be the judge of that!

—◌ ◌—

Something to Think About

Christianity is not illogical or irrational—the philosophers are.

> I want a principle within of watchful, godly fear,
> A sensibility of sin, A pain to feel it near.
> Help me the first approach to feel
> Of pride or wrong desire,
> To catch the wandering of my will
> And quench the kindling fire.
>
> —"I Want a Principle Within"

—◌ ◌—

Something to Do

Study Colossians 2:6–15. Take the warning to heart.

87

Celebrate!

> But if Christ is in you, your body is dead because of
> sin, yet your spirit is alive because of righteousness.
> And if the Spirit of him who raised Jesus from the
> dead is living in you, he who raised Christ from the
> dead will also give life to your mortal bodies through
> his Spirit, who lives in you.
>
> —Romans 8:10–11

What makes life tolerable? What banishes death and the fear connected with it? It's not doctrinal or philosophical theology, not prophetic interpretation, and not the doctrine of the Second Advent. What banishes the fear of death is the person of the risen Christ. Because Jesus Christ is *alive*, all the philosophical, logical, and religious arguments against Christianity disintegrate. Because he lives, all the arguments of the world are nonsense. Because he came out of the tomb *immortal*, death will be swallowed up by life.

Because Jesus Christ is alive, all the philosophical, logical, and religious arguments against Christianity disintegrate.

Do you know, you can't talk about Christmas without celebrating the Resurrection? When you're talking about the baby that came *into* the world by God the Holy Spirit, you've got to talk about the man who was raised up *from* the world by God the Holy Spirit.

I'll tell you something: I'm going to be so glad to trade in this carcass for that immortal body! I'm going to be so glad to enter at last into the presence of peace that knows no description, joy that is inexpressible, and victory that is ours by grace. The Christian can rejoice in Jesus Christ because he is a *living* Savior. Buddha, Mohammed, Confucius, Zoroaster, and all the philosophers of earth share one common factor: They're all dead! There isn't one of them that made it back. But Jesus Christ's gospel has been propelled for almost two thousand years by one fact—he lives!

The empirical and scientific proof that he lives is the fact that he transforms the lives of people: He takes the drug addict, he takes the prostitute, he takes the disgruntled and the downtrodden; he takes the proud and the arrogant; he takes *what* you are and *where* you are, and with the touch of divine grace he transforms you and re-creates you. There are no retreads with God—only re-creations.

The acid proof of Christianity was not the prophecies of the Old Testament. The acid proof of Christianity was not the forensic debating capacities of the apostles. It was not the good lives led or even the miracles performed. The acid proof and test of Christianity was whether or not Jesus Christ could conquer death. Every living person knows they must die. The death rate is still one per person. You're going to meet it and I'm going to meet it, if Jesus Christ does not come back in our lifetime.

But what banishes the fear of death? What makes life tolerable? The person of the *living* Christ. *He is alive,* and he has conquered death!

Something to Think About

How often do you celebrate the Resurrection?

> *Death cannot keep his prey,*
> *Jesus, my Savior!*
> *He tore the bars away,*
> *Jesus, my Lord!*
>
> *Up from the grave He arose,*
> *With a mighty triumph o'er His foes;*
> *He arose a victor from the dark domain,*
> *And He lives forever with His saints to reign:*
> *He arose! He arose!*
> *Hallelujah! Christ arose!*
>   —"Low in the Grave He Lay"

Something to Do

Rejoice in Jesus Christ because he is a *living* Savior.

88

I've Got Legs!

Now a man crippled from birth was being carried to the temple gate called Beautiful, where he was put every day to beg from those going into the temple courts. When he saw Peter and John about to enter, he asked them for money. Peter looked straight at him, as did John. Then Peter said, "Look at us!" So the man gave them his attention, expecting to get something from them.

Then Peter said, "Silver or gold I do not have, but what I have I give you. In the name of Jesus Christ of Nazareth, walk." Taking him by the right hand, he helped him up, and instantly the man's feet and ankles became strong. He jumped to his feet and began to walk. Then he went with them into the temple courts, walking and jumping, and praising God.

—Acts 3:2–8

A few years ago, I experienced something I believed could *never* happen to me. I was a philosophical theologian—I'm still a philosophical theologian—but now I'm a theologian who believes in the ministry of the Holy Spirit.

The Lord brought me to this belief in a miraculous way. I knew the answers theologically and apologetically, but *experientially* I'd never seen the evidence that Jesus Christ is alive. Someone may say,

"Well, every newborn soul is evidence." Of course, it is, but to the person who's philosophically oriented you want more evidence than just a testimony.

I was in New England at the time and I happened to be preaching in a church out near Cape Cod. It had been a very hard week, and I felt dead tired. I decided not to preach any more that week; I wanted to go home and rest. On my way back to New Jersey, I stopped to visit a friend, who was also a pastor. We chatted for a while and as I was leaving, he said, "Oh, by the way, Walter, I'm going to a very special meeting tonight—they're all converted drug addicts. Would you like to come?"

"*No*, thank you," I smiled and shook my head. "I'm just too tired."

"Look, you don't have to preach," he argued "Just come and sit there and enjoy the meeting. It's a great testimony."

"I'm tired and *I don't want to go*," I answered, as nicely as possible under the circumstances. (I was so exhausted, I couldn't think of anything else to say.)

"You'll get blessed!" he promised.

"*Oh, all right*—I'll go." This guy wouldn't give up! I was beat, but I needed to be blessed.

So I went. He told me, "I give you my word, Doc, you don't have to preach."

You know, you meet people like this in life: They give you their word that you won't have to do something, then they get you to do something *else*—very sneaky people. When we arrived he casually said, "You don't have to preach tonight, Walt, but maybe you'd like to give a testimony?" I gave my testimony, and I spoke of how the Lord had touched my life and shown me some things about the Spirit of God and how I praised him for it.

After the service, I slipped down the left aisle of the auditorium and headed straight for a side exit hidden behind some curtains. I walked out the door, and as I came down the back steps, a nice-looking boy, about seventeen years of age, awaited me at the bottom of the stairs. When I saw him, I thought, *How sad! A handsome, healthy young man—leaning on crutches.*

"Sir," he addressed me, very quietly. "Would you do me a favor?"

"What is it?" I asked.

"I heard you say that you believe Jesus can heal."

"I do."

"Would you pray for me?"

In that instant, I *panicked,* and looked around for help (being at heart a man of great faith).

"Uh, well," I stammered, still looking for help. (There wasn't anyone around!) I had just talked about Acts 3:6, so what could I do? I gave in, "All right. I'll pray for you."

I laid my hands on him and just before I started to pray, one person came out the door—a Roman Catholic nun wearing the Holy Spirit emblem of a dove. She was a charismatic! *Oh well,* I thought, *I need all the help I can get.*

I began to pray. Oh, did I pray! "Lord touch this boy. Lord heal him." I didn't know what was the matter with him, except that he had crutches.

We finished and I asked him how he felt. He replied, "I don't rightly know. But I feel like I've got legs!"

"Like you have *what*?"

"Legs!" he shouted.

"Don't you have any legs?" I said, stunned.

"Yes, Sir. But I have steel braces on my legs because *I've never walked.* My legs are atrophied, and I can't feel anything."

"What do you feel now?"

"I feel like I've got legs!"

I'm such a great man of faith. I turned around to two buckskinned brothers who were standing there, complete with beards, and I motioned, "Come over here, Brothers."

They stood on either side of him, and he handed me his crutches. I said, "If Jesus touched you, you can walk." He walked! He walked toward me and threw his arms around me and kissed me. He walked all over that auditorium. He walked up and down the stairs eight times. He walked across the parking lot, and I had to stop him from walking home! Later I found out he walked until four o'clock in the morning, because he was afraid if he stopped walking, he'd never walk again.

God showed me for the first time that night the *experiential* evidence that Jesus Christ is alive. The power of the Holy Spirit is as real today as it was two thousand years ago when the Apostle Peter said, "Walk." God had healed this young man and, in the process, he'd touched my heart in a way that would forever change my life.

The power of the Holy Spirit is as real today as it was two thousand years ago when the Apostle Peter said, "Walk."

Something to Think About

God brings us to belief.

> My great Physician heals the sick,
> The lost He came to save;
> For me His precious blood He shed,
> For me His life He gave.
>
> I need no other argument,
> I need no other plea;
> It is enough that Jesus died,
> And that He died for me.
> —"My Faith Has Found A Resting Place"

Something to Do

Ask God to show you the experiential evidence that Jesus Christ is alive.

89

Focus

No one serving as a soldier gets involved in civilian affairs—he wants to please his commanding officer.
—2 Timothy 2:4

In this passage Paul instructs us to look at the soldier in normal training and in combat. A soldier does not get involved in civilian pursuits in order to please his commanding officer. In the same way *you* are a soldier. Don't get involved in the pursuits of the world and you'll be able to please Christ, who has called you to be his soldier.

This isn't saying you can't become involved in politics, government, and education. It tells you not to get caught up in anything that will *detract* from your service to Christ—no matter what it is. That doesn't mean you don't get entangled at all. It means you don't get involved to the degree that it cripples you and you're unable to perform your function as a soldier of the cross.

Avoid distraction. Don't let anything get in the way of your focal point of concentration. What is your focal point of concentration? Survival. A soldier must survive. General Patton put it far more eloquently then I ever could—but I will not use his language. The general said, "You don't win wars by dying for your country. You win wars by getting the *other guy* to die for *his* country." That's common sense. You need to know your Scripture so thoroughly that cultic distortion and misinterpretation cannot stand against your argument. It is *their* theology, *their* faith which should be shaken to its very roots—and eventually, to *death*.

If you want to be victorious, you must have God's power to conquer. How do you get it? "Do your best to present yourself to God as one approved, a workman who does not need to be ashamed and who correctly handles the word of truth" (2 Tim. 2:15). Study God's Word, pray for his power, focus on him above all else—and then stand and fight.

If you want to be victorious, you must have God's power to conquer.

Something to Think About

Don't let anything get in the way of your focal point of concentration.

Teach me to love thee as thine angels love,
One holy passion filling all my frame;
The baptism of the heav'n-descended Dove,
My heart an altar and thy love the flame.
—"Spirit of God, Descend upon My Heart"

Something to Do

Study God's Word, pray for his power, focus on him above all else—and then stand and fight.

90

Guts

Therefore, get rid of all moral filth and the evil that is so prevalent and humbly accept the word planted in you, which can save you.

Do not merely listen to the word, and so deceive yourselves. Do what it says. Anyone who listens to the word but does not do what it says is like a man who looks at his face in a mirror and, after looking at himself, goes away and immediately forgets what he looks like.

—James 1:21–24

What has happened to American ethics? We have forgotten the God and the revelation that gave us the ethical structure upon which we built. By turning away from him, we are automatically turning away from the values that proceeded from union with him. Thus the disintegration of ethics and morality. That's why you can say, "Well if it works for me, fine. If it works for you, fine. If it doesn't hurt anyone else, do it." Lie, cheat, steal, murder your children, do whatever is necessary as long as you don't violate anyone else's rights—as if a child doesn't have any right to live. Can you see the next step? Euthanasia. If you can kill the fruit of the womb, you can kill the womb itself.

> *By turning away from God, we are automatically turning away from the values that proceeded from union with him.*

223

I talked about this on tape a few years ago, and when we released it at Christian Research Institute some of my friends said, "Don't you think you're going a little too *far* with this?" If I had to do the tape over again, I would have gone *farther*. Right now, it is the murder of the children; in the gathering storm, it's going to be the murder of *you*. You will have the right to decide your own suicide—your own death. If the State can permit you to kill your child, the state can permit you to kill yourself. It is a very foolish person who doesn't see the logical connection.

If I sound concerned, I am. You must have zeal for the Word of God. You must have what so many do not have—guts. The Christian church *must* speak out against evil. If we don't, we become guilty.

Pope Pious XII sat on his hands in the Vatican and let six million Jews go to the gas chamber—he never said a word. That's history. He knew it and he never said a word. That made him an accessory to murder. He died screaming for forgiveness from God for the agony he had not tried to interrupt. Most people don't know that, but it's true.

If you keep quiet in the presence of evil, you're guilty. You are as guilty as the person doing it because *you will not speak*. Today, we have forgotten God and his revelation. American ethics and morals are disintegrating and the Church *must* be heard!

—⟨⟩ ⟨⟩—

Something to Think About

You must have zeal for the Word of God. You must have what so many do not have—guts.

> *May Thy rich grace impart*
> *Strength to my fainting heart,*
> *My zeal inspire;*
> *As Thou hast died for me,*
> *O may my love to thee*
> *Pure, warm, and change-less be,*
> *A living fire!*
> —"My Faith Looks Up to Thee"

—⟨⟩ ⟨⟩—

Something to Do

The Christian church must speak out against evil. If we don't, we become guilty. God calls you to his service; seek wisdom and courage to answer the call.

91

~◌₃ ◌₃~

The Cup of Fellowship

> *"My soul is overwhelmed with sorrow to the point of death," he said to them. "Stay here and keep watch."*
> *Going a little farther, he fell to the ground and prayed that if possible the hour might pass from him. "Abba, Father," he said, "everything is possible for you. Take this cup from me. Yet not what I will, but what you will."*
>
> —Mark 14:34–36

Calvary did not sneak up on Jesus of Nazareth. He had prophesied repeatedly that the Son of Man must be delivered into the hands of sinful men; he must go to Jerusalem, he must suffer many things from the chief priest and the Scribes, and he must die and rise the third day.

The core of a great spiritual truth of the Easter season is something we often fail to see. Do you remember when Jesus prayed in the Garden of Gethsemane? "'Abba, Father,' he said, 'everything is possible for you. Take this cup from me. Yet not what I will, but what you will'" (Mark 14:36). Some theologians have said that in this verse Jesus displayed true humanity. He was frightened at the prospect of imprisonment, punishment, and death, just like any of us would be. And so he cried out, "Father! If there is a way for me to avoid this, let it be so."

That's *not* what it says. What is the cup? It's *not* the cup of suffering because Jesus said he'd been born to this end. He knew all the things that would happen to him. What is the meaning of that cup? If you study your Bible, you'll find out that it's the cup of *fellowship*.

225

The cup is the symbol of union.

This cup is a very important cup. It is the symbol of union. What Jesus meant was this: "If it's possible for me, Father, to go through the hell of Calvary and not break my fellowship with you, please let it be."

Do you know what the agony of the cross was? Not just the physical suffering for your sins and mine, and the spiritual anguish of rejection, but it was the absolute *horror* of suddenly being separated from the cup of fellowship Jesus had with his Father from all eternity. Jesus said, "Oh please, Father, if I can just maintain fellowship . . ." The Father said, "No. You can't maintain fellowship, but you will never be left alone."

The Father looked upon the Son as the sin offering for the world. Contrary to popular evangelistic fervor, he did not turn his back on Jesus and walk away. No, he studiously looked upon the suffering of his Son and realized, in the agony of himself and Christ, that there was a separation of fellowship between them. For God cannot tolerate the presence of evil, and Christ—who knew no sin—was made to become sin for us, that we might be made as righteous as God by faith in him. That's the cup that Jesus did not want to have to endure—the moment when the Father and he would be in a *separation* of fellowship. Scripture gives us this lesson so we will never, ever underestimate the suffering of the cross.

—⚬ ⚬—

Something to Think About

What is the cup of fellowship?

> *Upon that cross of Jesus*
> *Mine eyes at times can see*
> *The very dying form of One*
> *Who suffered there for me;*
> *And from my smitten heart with tears*
> *Two wonders I confess—*
> *The wonders of His glorious love*
> *And my unworthiness.*
> —"Beneath the Cross of Jesus"

—⚬ ⚬—

Something to Do

Envision the suffering of the cross.

92

Ultimate Power

"Do you refuse to speak to me?" Pilate said. "Don't you realize I have power either to free you or to crucify you?" Jesus answered, "You would have no power over me if it were not given to you from above."
—John 19:10–11

When Pontius Pilate demanded that Jesus answer him, Jesus told him, "You don't have any power at all." All the air must have gone out of Pilate's balloon! The ultimate power rested with the one who stood before Pilate, not with Pilate sitting on his little marble throne. Pontius Pilate, his throne, his palace, Jerusalem, and even the Roman Empire is known today as "stick and stone-ology"—the study of archeology—it's *gone*, it's history, it's forever over.

But the Word of God and the Church of Jesus Christ, against which the gates of hell have never been able to prevail, remain constant to this day. It towers over the wreck of Caesar and of Judaism as it towers over all the wrecks of time, because it cannot be touched by time! Time cannot touch an immortal man. Time cannot touch *deathlessness*. Time cannot touch him who has the power of *indestructible, imperishable life* (Hebrews 7:16).

Jesus Christ in his resurrection is imperishably alive. Time, decay, and everything that you and I have to live through and endure cannot touch him. He has offered one sacrifice for sin, forever, and sat down at the right hand of God—expecting

One sacrifice for sin, forever.

and anticipating that his enemies will be kneeling before him, with his foot on their necks.

Pontius Pilate thought he possessed all the power, but across from him sat the man who possessed the *ultimate* power. His enemies will be his footstool.

—❧ ❧—

Something to Think About

The ultimate power rests with God.

> *Will you evade Him as Pilate tried?*
> *Or will you choose Him, whate'er betide?*
> *Vainly you struggle from Him to hide:*
> *What will you do with Jesus?*

> *What will you do with Jesus?*
> *Neutral you cannot be;*
> *Someday your heart will be asking:*
> *"What will He do with me?"*
>   — "What Will You Do with Jesus?"

—❧ ❧—

Something to Do

Study Matthew 5:14–16. What will you do with Jesus?

93

The Messiah

Then the Jews demanded of him, "What miraculous
sign can you show us to prove your authority to do all
this?" Jesus answered them, "Destroy this temple, and
I will raise it again in three days." The Jews replied,
"It has taken forty-six years to build this temple, and
you are going to raise it in three days?" But the tem-
ple he had spoken of was his body. After he was raised
from the dead, his disciples recalled what he had said.
Then they believed the Scripture and the words that
Jesus had spoken.

—John 2:18–22

Jesus prophesied his resurrection. He even prophesied the nature of
his resurrection. "Destroy this temple, and I will raise it again in three
days." The prophecy of his bodily resurrection is the foundation of all
Christian theology. Without its fulfillment, he was a liar, a false
prophet. He was deservedly executed and Deuteronomy 13 could be
applied to him without question.

If Jesus is really the Messiah, then he is—in the true, classic sense
of prophetic fulfillment—a person with enormous power. Not just
charisma, but a person with enormous power. The Old Testament
record revealed in Daniel 8 and 9 that the Messiah would die—but
not for *himself*. He would die for the sins of the people. He would be
the conqueror, and David said it would not be possible that death

should hold him hostage. This is more than just an earthly ruler. This is someone with enormous power. We're talking about the Redeemer; we're talking about the Conqueror of Death. We're talking about someone who died not for himself, but for the sins of all mankind.

Christianity is the exclusive way to heaven. Why? Because Jesus Christ rose from the dead. If he didn't rise from the dead, he was a phony: He was a false messiah, a false prophet, a liar, a deceiver, and demon possessed—at the very worst.

If he rose from the dead, as the Scripture says, then he is the Son of God with *power*, because of his resurrection. He is the way, the truth, and the life, because no one else could rise from the dead and no one else could conquer death as he did. His unique claim to everything is by virtue of his resurrection. Therefore, he is the Son of God. He is the Savior of the World, and that's why Christianity is the truth.

> *Christianity is the exclusive way to heaven. Why? Because Jesus Christ rose from the dead.*

Our faith rests on the Resurrection. More than five hundred eyewitnesses testified to seeing Jesus *after* his resurrection—including the Apostle Paul who was *not* a believer at that time. If you presented this in any courtroom, you could prove any case you wanted to—it's *evidence*. But there is also the fact that Jesus Christ saves people. When he saves you, he transforms you, and only a living Savior can transform the lives of people. He's been doing that for almost two thousand years.

The Resurrection is the confirmation of the ministry of the Lord Jesus. He is the Messiah. Jesus said, "But if I do it, even though you do not believe me, believe the miracles, that you may know and understand that the Father is in me, and I in the Father" (John 10:38). What greater work could there be than this—after having died physically, he should raise himself from the dead? Jesus said *he* would raise his body up. He didn't say, "Destroy this body and my Father will raise me up." He didn't say, "Destroy this body and the Holy Spirit will raise me up." He said, "*I* will raise it up." That was an affirmation of *divinity* because it meant "I will conquer death." He is Messiah, son of David. He is the King Messiah.

—⚬ ⚬—

Something to Think About

When Jesus Christ saves you, he transforms you.

The Church's one foundation
Is Jesus Christ her Lord;
She is His new creation
By water and the Word:
From heaven He came and sought her
To be His holy bride;
With His own blood He bought her,
And for her life He died.
'Mid toil and tribulation,
And tumult of her war,
She waits the consummation
Of peace forevermore;
Till, with the vision glorious,
Her longing eyes are blest,
And the great Church victorious
Shall be the Church at rest.
                    —"The Church's One Foundation"

Something to Do

Take a moment and write a few words on Christ's resurrection. What does it mean to you?

94

The Difference

Whatever happens, conduct yourselves in a manner worthy of the gospel of Christ. Then, whether I come and see you or only hear about you in my absence, I will know that you stand firm in one spirit, contending as one man for the faith of the gospel.
—Philippians 1:27

God often uses people who are not believers to help us in times of need. I can remember a special friend I had long ago—he was an Orthodox Jew who ran a restaurant in New York City right down the street from where I was going to school. I was finishing my senior year of college, and I didn't have much money—I'd actually lost fifty pounds because I couldn't eat regularly. Even with my mother helping me, and trying to pick up some work on the side, being a student was murder back in the 1950s.

Well, this gentleman was a retired prize fighter who'd gone into the restaurant business. He and I became friends because of our mutual love of boxing, and we would sit around and discuss the great fights of the century, and so forth. This continued for quite a while until, inevitably, I ran out of money. I couldn't make it in there for a few weeks, but when I finally dropped by for a cup of coffee, he was waiting for me.

He came right over to my table and asked me, "Where have you been, Doc?"

"Well, uh," I replied, embarrassed, "I haven't been able to come in, Sid, because I don't have any money."

"You don't have any money!" he exclaimed. in a *very loud* voice. "Come with me!" And he took me to the back of his store.

We went into his office, and he took out a book from the drawer and wrote my name at the top of the page. He said, "You eat as much as you want, as often as you want, and as long as you want until you finish the year. If you still need help, let me know. No friend of mine is going to go hungry."

I was amazed! I had witnessed to Sid many times, and he didn't believe the gospel. "I'll pay you back, of course." I said. "That's very gracious of you. But how can you be sure you can trust me?"

"I know the difference."

He looked at me for a long moment and then answered, "Because you're a Christian, and I know the *difference*."

One of the joys of my life, after I got my first job and was attending graduate school, was to go back and hand Sid a check. When he took the check he said, "Are you sure you don't need this, Doc?"

I smiled and replied, "No, I'm fine. Wonderful. Thank you!"

He fed me, literally, for a year. Now that was a fulfillment of Jesus' instructions to us to be friendly with the people around us—not for what they can give to us—but for the purpose of witnessing to them. People need to hear the gospel and friends often have the opportunity to share it. One of the side benefits of our friendship was that God used Sid to help me at a time when I was in need.

I always delight in telling this story because I witnessed to Sid many times, and I hope someday he'll be in the kingdom of God. He was a very gracious man.

―――

Something to Think About

People need to hear the gospel, and friends often have the opportunity to share it.

> Standing on the promises of Christ my King,
> Thru eternal ages let His praises ring;
> Glory in the highest, I will shout and sing,
> Standing on the promises of God.

> Standing on the promises that cannot fail,
> When the howling storms of doubt and fear assail,

By the living Word of God I shall prevail,
Standing on the promises of God.
—"Standing on the Promises"

_⸰ ⸰_

Something to Do

Proverbs 17:17 speaks of the meaning of true friendship. Study it carefully. What kind of a friend are you?

95

Simplicity

If you point these things out to the brothers, you will be a good minister of Christ Jesus, brought up in the truths of the faith and of the good teaching that you have followed.

—1 Timothy 4:6

What does it take to be a good servant, a good minister, a good witness for Jesus Christ? Has God given us any guidelines?

Yes, but you can give marvelous sermons and tremendous illustrations; you can spellbind audiences, thump your Bible, pound the pulpit, manipulate vocabulary—and miss the whole point. *Simplicity.* God wants us to translate our theology, our doctrine, and our faith into our walk, our witness, and our life.

The Pharisees were renowned for having the epitome of sound doctrine. The scribes were cited by Christ as having great righteousness that came from their observance of the letter of the Law. In fact, Jesus said unless your righteousness exceeds the righteousness of the Pharisees and the scribes, you can't enter the kingdom of God. And yet with all of their knowledge, all of their zeal, and all their religiosity, they had missed the point: The translation of the Law of Moses from the *letter* to the *spirit*—and the living of that in one's life.

If you tried to live the Law of Moses by the letter, you had 622 laws to live by, and you would have needed a pocket calculator to keep up with all of them. That's why they had the morning and evening sacrifices: the morning sacrifices for the things you missed during the night, and the evening sacrifices for the things you missed during the day. God knew the impossibility of perfection on the part of men. The *purpose* of the Law was to reveal your imperfection, so that you would trust the grace of God and have faith in his goodness to redeem you.

So Paul, in a pastoral epistle to young Timothy, writes, "You know, doctrine is very important. If you pursue it and are consistent in it, you save yourself and others by the teachings. But," says Paul, "if you really want to accomplish that goal, then that doctrine needs to translate into how you live." And so he got right down to the nitty-gritty with young Timothy in communicating what he had to do to be a good minister of Christ, a good witness, and a good servant.

How do you become an effective voice for Christ? How do you excel as a servant of the Lord Jesus? The first thing you must do is to recognize the times in which you live. Don't live in a fool's paradise. The Church is not going to usher in the kingdom of God. The Church is going to be *rescued* by the coming of the kingdom of God. That's what's going to save us—and we're going to *need* saving at that particular point in history, because the Scripture says the whole world will be dominated by the forces of darkness.

> How do you become an effective voice for Christ? How do you excel as a servant of the Lord Jesus?

The last days are with us. They've been here for nineteen hundred plus years. If you want to be a good servant of Jesus Christ, you must tell the Church what the true condition of the world is; you must tell the Church what her *own* true condition is. In effect, Paul instructed Timothy, "Tell it like it is and let the chips fall where they may. You are not responsible for the falling of the chips, you are only responsible for telling people the truth."

The task of every pastor, every evangelist, every person in leadership in the Christian church, and every witness for the Lord Jesus is not to float along *with* the tide of the world, but to vigorously *resist it,* because the world is under the dominion of satanic power. The proof of your Christian pudding, your nourishment in the words of faith and good teaching, is vigorously—and without compromise—stating the truth. If you do that, the truth will set you free.

No matter what type of witnessing strategy you come up with— no matter how forensic your presentation or how brilliant the apologetics—when you're finally finished people are still going to be either skeptics, procrastinators, or believers. These are the three categories we find repeatedly in the ministry of our Lord and in the ministries of the apostles and disciples.

We should, therefore, not be discouraged when people turn away from the good news of the Resurrection. What we ought to do is be sure that *we* do a good job in answering the objections. One plants, another waters, and the Lord gives the increase. We are planting and watering. Be sure you do a good job of it.

Something to Think About

Christians do not float along with the tide—they vigorously *resist* it.

Fierce may be the conflict, Strong may be the foe,
But the King's own army, None can overthrow;
Round His standard ranging, Victory is secure,
For His truth unchanging makes the triumph sure.

Joyfully enlisting, By Thy grace divine,
We are on the Lord's side—
Savior, we are Thine!

—"Who Is on the Lord's Side?"

Something to Do

God wants us to translate our theology, our doctrine, and our faith into our walk, our witness, and our life.

96

_⟶ ᴄ⟩ ᴄ⟩_

Fleece or Fur?

"I tell you the truth, the man who does not enter the sheep pen by the gate, but climbs in by some other way, is a thief and a robber. The man who enters by the gate is the shepherd of his sheep. The watchman opens the gate for him, and the sheep listen to his voice. He calls his own sheep by name and leads them out. When he has brought out all his own, he goes on ahead of them, and his sheep follow him because they know his voice."

—John 10:1–4

Christ, as the good Shepherd, is the one who *identifies* the sheep. He is the one who calls the sheep—it is a personal invitation. He calls his sheep by name and when he leads them out, he goes before them. You do not walk alone in the world, Jesus Christ walks before you if you are one of his sheep.

The emphasis here is very clear. What does a shepherd do? He leads, feeds, tends, and defends the flock. And the sheep listen to their shepherd's voice. Christians—sheep—may be led astray by false doctrine and false teaching, but they always know the voice of the Master. You can never be happy, contented, or at peace in your sins. Never. You can fall into sin, be led astray or be deceived, but your coat is *wool*—fleece, not fur—and when the Shepherd calls, you know his voice and you

You can never be happy, contented, or at peace in your sins. Never.

238

are not comfortable until you respond. That's what separates goats from sheep: The goats just go on their way, and the sheep hear the voice of the Shepherd. Jesus said, "If you really are my sheep, no matter where you are or what you're doing, when you hear my voice, you'll listen."

―◌ ◌―

Something to Think About

You do not walk alone in the world; Jesus Christ walks before you if you are one of his sheep.

> *Take the name of Jesus with you,*
> *Child of sorrow and of woe;*
> *It will joy and comfort give you,*
> *Take it then where 'er you go*
>
> *Take the name of Jesus ever*
> *As a shield from every snare;*
> *When if temptations round you gather,*
> *Breathe that holy name in prayer.*
>
> *Precious name, O how sweet!*
> *Hope of earth and joy of heaven;*
> *Precious name, O how sweet!*
> *Hope of earth and joy of heaven.*
> —"Take the Name of Jesus with You"

―◌ ◌―

Something to Do

Explore Ezekiel 34. Rest in the word of the Lord.

97

_◌ ◌_

Peace with God

*Then you will know the truth, and the truth will set
you free.*

—John 8:32

The playboy philosophy of hedonism or the "new morality" can
never be described as anything new. The apostle Paul talked about it
almost two thousand years ago (1 Cor. 15:32).

The philosophy before us is this: You go through this life only
once, so grab anything you can get your hands on now. There are all
kinds of exponents of this philosophy of the new morality and situation ethics. Whatever situation you find yourself in, you pragmati-
cally apply the ethic to get you out of it. There is no absolute ethic.
There is no absolute morality. So, situation ethics and the new morality are summed up under one word: *relativism*. Relative truth, relative
morality, relative ethics. There is no absolute God. There is no
absolute morality. There is no absolute ethic. It is all relativism.
Everything is relevant to the culture and the time. The Christian must
be prepared to give an answer to this.

The people who speak of relativism and situation ethics have a
very difficult time with many very difficult problems. You *must* go to
an absolute to judge Hitler and Stalin. You must go to an absolute, if
you're a relativist, to make a moral judgment when men are exploited
and murdered. You have to do it because your relativism can't help
you. *You don't have any authority.*

As soon as relativism negates authority, *experience* becomes authority—and as soon as experience becomes authority, you have concentration camps and all the rest of it. When people blindly claim a relativistic view, they are really committing themselves to philosophical and historical suicide. If we apply the same standard, we could never sit in judgment over the tyrants of earth—whom we obviously have judged by destroying them.

> **When people blindly claim a relativistic view, they are committing themselves to philosophical and historical suicide.**

Only in revelation is there the establishment of an *absolute* that will endure throughout all time. The contemporary challenges to Christianity are no more successful in the end than their ancestors have been. What Jesus Christ said was indeed, as always, an absolute truth, "Then you will know the truth, and the truth will set you free" (John 8:32). No man can know the truth unless he has made peace with God, for the answer to Pontius Pilate's question, "What is truth?" (John 18:38) is resolved only in the person of Jesus Christ. Truth was standing right in front of Pilate! What is truth? "I am the way and the truth and the life. No one comes to the Father except through me" (John 14:6).

―∽ ∾―

Something to Think About

Only in revelation is there the establishment of an *absolute* that will endure throughout all time.

> *How firm a foundation, ye saints of the Lord*
> *Is laid for your faith in His excellent Word!*
> *What more can He say than to you He has said—*
> *To you, who for refuge to Jesus have fled?*
>
> *"Fear not, I am with thee—O be not dismayed,*
> *For I am thy God, I will still give thee aid;*
> *I'll strengthen thee, help thee, and cause thee to stand,*
> *Upheld by my gracious, omnipotent hand."*
> —*I'll never, no never, no never forsake!"*

―∽ ∾―

Something to Do

Review this teaching and study the arguments against the philosophy of relativism.

98

Pet Theories

"For sighing comes to me instead of food;
my groans pour out like water.
What I feared has come upon me;
what I dreaded has happened to me.
I have no peace, no quietness;
I have no rest, but only turmoil."

—Job 3:24–26

Some preachers today are set on misinterpreting Job's words, "What I feared has come upon me." I wish they would take the time to read the first chapter of Job, where it says that *Satan* was the cause of Job's trouble. Satan came into the presence of God and said, "Give him to me and he'll curse you to your face" (Job 1:11). That was *before* anything happened to Job. They don't know what they're talking about when they try to blame this on Job's fear. That is not what the passage says.

In addition to this misinterpretation, they speculate that Job was continually offering burnt sacrifices because he *expected* all this to happen to him. This error occurs when you don't have any theological education. Burnt offerings were part of sacrifices made to God for the express purpose of *taking care of sin*. Job offered a burnt offering for his children's sins as well as his own, just in case the kids forgot to confess to God (1:5). If you read it in English or Hebrew, you couldn't miss it. The problem is, these people superimpose their own theories on Scripture, and they end up with this kind of nonsense.

242

People sometimes say to me, "Why do you get so irritated when this happens?" Because when you are teaching theology and biblical studies, *you are responsible for the souls of the people who listen to you.* I am responsible to God, as a teacher, for what I teach you because he set me in the Church as a teacher. I do not have any right to give you my pet theories, without identifying them as such. I don't have any right to give you far-out, off-the-wall theological garbage, just because it happens to be something I think is true. I have a responsibility to teach you what the text says, and with the best scholarship I can get my hands on, to give you a well-rounded picture. You're supposed to take what I teach you and apply it in your life, *after* you have tested it by the Word of God to find out if what I say is true. That's the methodology the teaching arm of the Church has always used.

Not so, today. Today, you have a bunch of evangelists with virtually no education, teaching theology to people who know even less than they do. It's the uninformed teaching the ignorant—sharing the abundance of *their* ignorance. And then what happens? Disaster! People need to speak out against this. People need to sit down and write letters. They need to get on the phone or send telegrams. They need to say, "I won't send you another dime." Money is a powerful incentive for change.

Somebody needs to say something! When you're teaching theology and biblical studies, you are responsible for the souls of the people who listen to you. Job's fear did not bring on disaster. God allowed him to be tested, and in the end, he blessed him greatly for his faithfulness.

Somebody needs to say something!

Something to Think About

Job's fear did not bring disaster.

> *I would be true,*
> *for there are those who trust me;*
> *I would be pure,*
> *for there are those who care;*
> *I would be strong,*
> *for there is much to suffer;*
> *I would be brave,*
> *for there is much to dare,*

I would be brave,
for there is much to dare.
              —"I Would Be True"

Something to Do

Take what teachers tell you, myself included, and apply it in your life, *after* you have tested it by the Word of God to confirm that what we say is true.

99

_⌒⊱ ⊰⌒_

Finding God

For it is written:
"I will destroy the wisdom of the wise;
the intelligence of the intelligent I will frustrate."
—1 Corinthians 1:19

With all the wisdom the Greeks had, with all the wisdom the Egyptians had, with all the wisdom of all the cultures of mankind in its totality—they never found God. The golden age of Greece led them to Plato's Republic, to utter disaster, to moral chaos, and to multiple polytheistic worship. That was the golden age of Greece. The summit of man's wisdom led him to despair.

You know, we're in a world like that today. People all over the place are advertising, "You can find God!" Get into meditation and you can find God. Cross your legs and contemplate a rock, a flower, and a cup of water in Zen and you can find God. Dash off to a corner meeting with Jehovah's Witnesses; run into the theocratic kingdom and you will find God. Go to the Mormons and you will find God. Or better yet—join a spiritualistic séance to contact Aunt Patty and you will find God. Never before in the history of mankind have there been so many people running around the landscape saying, "Here! Here! Here is God!" And no one has found him yet.

The summit of man's wisdom led him to despair.

Is it because he isn't there? Of course not. It's because *he's not going to be found* except by the methodology which he has described. It's as clear in the revelation of God as could be. Jesus said, "I am the way and the truth and the life. No one comes to the Father except through me" (John 14:6). This is the simple truth of the gospel. The world by its own wisdom couldn't get itself arrested. It couldn't find out anything about God.

Something to Think About

"The fear of the LORD is the beginning of wisdom; all who follow his precepts have good understandings" (Ps. 111:10)

> *My soul, be on thy guard;*
> *Ten thousand foes arise;*
> *The hosts of sin are pressing hard*
> *To draw thee to the skies.*
>
> *O watch and fight and pray;*
> *The battle never give o'er;*
> *Renew it boldly every day,*
> *And help divine implore*
>   —"My Soul, Be on Thy Guard"

Something to Do

What is the simple truth of the gospel? Commit John 14:6 to memory.

100

_◌ ◌_

The Victory

*For everyone born of God overcomes the world. This
is the victory that has overcome the world, even our
faith. Who is it that overcomes the world? Only he
who believes that Jesus is the Son of God.*

—1 John 5:4–5

How do you get the power of God to conquer? You get the power of
God by a very simple biblical method which most people are dead-
on determined to ignore—because it's so simple! Do you think that
spiritual warfare and the ultimate victory are *hard*? No. The promise
of God is the simplest thing in the world to accept, and one of the
most difficult for mankind because we're always trying to win the battle for ourselves.

The Lord says, "I've got news for you. I have the ultimate solution." Are you ready? The final conquest is 1 John 5:4–5. Here it is!
This is the victory that conquers the world—our faith! You may say,
"*That's* something new and startling?" It is when you put it in its
proper context. What is faith? "Now faith is being sure of what we
hope for and certain of what we do not see" (Heb. 11:1). Think about
that for a second. How in the world do you get this kind of faith? *You
don't*, not by yourself! You can't ever get to the state of being sure of
what you hope for and certain of what you cannot see, unless God
gives you the measure of faith. God gives the measure of faith to every
person as it pleases him, not in proportion to your efforts, but as it

God gives you the power to conquer by giving you the measure of faith you need everyday.

pleases him. God gives you the power to conquer by giving you *the measure of faith you need everyday.* If we go to him and ask for the power, it is available for us whenever and wherever we may need it. *"This is the victory that has overcome the world, even our faith."*

Something to Think About

The promise of God is the simplest thing in the world to accept, and one of the most difficult for mankind because we're always trying to win the battle for ourselves.

His banner over us is love,
Our sword the Word of God;
We tread the road the saints above
With shouts of triumph trod.
By faith they, like a whirlwind's breath,
Swept on o'er every field;
The faith by which they conquer'd death
Is still our shining shield.

Faith is the victory!
Faith is the victory!
O glorious victory
That overcomes the world.

—"Faith Is the Victory"

Something to Do

How do you get the power of God to conquer? *Pray for faith.*

Bibliography

1. *The Baptism of Boldness*
2. *The Foolishness of God*
3. *Spiritual Warfare*
4. *The Foolishness of God*
5. Newport Mesa Christian Center Bible Class (NM), 11 January 1987
6. *Christianity in Crisis*
7. NM, 5 February 1989
8. *Christianity in Crisis*
9. *Christianity in Crisis*
10. *The Baptism of Boldness*
11. NM, 11 January 1987
12. *Spiritual Warfare*
13. NM, 8 February 1987
14. *The Baptism of Boldness*
15. NM, 1 January 1989
16. *The Foolishness of God*
17. *The Baptism of Boldness*
18. *The Doctrine of the Demons*
19. *The Health and Wealth Cult*, 15 July 1987
20. NM, 11 June 1989
21. *Jesus: God, Man or Myth?*
22. *The Baptism of Boldness*
23. NM, 21 May 19
24. *The Existence of Evil*
25. NM, 18 June 1989
26. NM, 4 January 1987
27. Ibid.
28. *The Baptism of Boldness*
29. *The Foolishness of God*

30. *The Foolishness of God*
31. *The Gospel of Eternity*
32. *The Health and Wealth Cult,* 15 July 1987
33. *The Way to Holiness*
34. *The Spirit of this Age*
35. *Reasons for Faith*
36. NM, 18 January 1987
37. *Reasons for Faith*
38. NM, 4 January 1987
39. *The Doctrine of the Demons*
40. *Christianity in Crisis*
41. NM, 5 February 1989
42. NM, 5 February 1989
43. *The Baptism of Boldness*
44. NM, 26 February 1989
45. NM, 26 February 1989
46. *The Doctrine of the Demons*
47. NM, 26 February 1989
48. NM, 19 February 1989
49. NM, 26 February 1989
50. *The Doctrine of the Demons*
51. *The Baptism of Boldness*
52. NM, 22 January 1989
53. NM, 22 January 1989
54. NM, 22 February 1987
55. NM, 8 February 1987
56. NM, 22 February 1987
57. NM, 1 January 1989
58. NM, 1 January 1989
59. NM, 1 January 1989
60. NM, 1 January 1989, and NM, 19 October 1986
61. NM, 4 January 1987, and NM, 28 February 1988
62. NM, 4 December 1988
63. *The Doctrine of the Demons*
64. *The Doctrine of the Demons*
65. NM, 22 February 1987
66. NM, 22 February 1987, and *The Health and Wealth Cult*
67. NM, 22 February 1987
68. NM, 1 January 1989
69. *The Doctrine of the Demons*

70. NM, 11 December 1988, and NM, 22 February 1987
71. NM, 18 June 1989
72. NM, 18 June 1989 and NM, 12 April 1987
73. NM, 18 June 1987
74. NM, 8 February 1987
75. *The Rise of the Cults*
76. NM, 11 January 1987
77. *The Gospel of the Resurrection*
78. NM, 27 March 1988
79. NM, 27 March 1988
80. NM, 27 March 1988
81. *Evangelism and Apologetics,* 2 December 1972
82. NM, 28 February 1988
83. NM, 28 February 1988
84. NM, 28 February 1988
85. *Jesus: God, Man or Myth*
86. *Jesus: God, Man or Myth* and NM, 11 June 1989
87. *Jesus: God, Man or Myth*
88. *Jesus: God, Man or Myth*
89. NM, 23 April 1989
90. *The Gathering Storm* and NM, 7 June 1987
91. NM, 12 April 1987
92. NM, 12 April 1987
93. NM, 12 April 1987 and NM, 11 June 1989
94. NM, 7 June 1987
95. NM, 7 June 1987 and *The Gospel of the Resurrection*
96. NM, 19 October 1986
97. *Reasons for Faith*
98. NM, 19 October 1986
99. Ibid.
100.*Spiritual Warfare*

Hymn Bibliography

1.   Reginald Herber and Henry S. Cutler, "The Son of God Goes Forth to War"

2.   Walter Chalmers Smith and Welsh Melody, "Immortal, Invisible"

3.   Sabine Baring-Gould and Arthur S. Sullivan, "Onward, Christian Soldiers"

4.   Will L. Thompson, "Softly and Tenderly"

5.   Frances R. Havergal and H. A. Cesar Malan, "Take My Life and Let It Be"

6.   Frances R. Havergal and C. Luise Reichardt, "Who Is on the Lord's Side?"

7.   George Croly and Frederick C. Atkinson, "Spirit of God, Descend upon My Heart"

8.   Washington Gladden and H. Percy-Smith, "O Master, Let Me Walk with Thee"

9.   Howard B. Grose and Charlotte A. Barnard, "Give of Your Best to the Master"

10.   William F. Sherwin, "Sound the Battle Cry!"

11.   Mary D. James and Source Unknown, "All for Jesus"

12.   Charles Wesley and George J. Elvey, "Soldiers of Christ, Arise"

13.   Cleland B. McAfee, "Near to the Heart of God"

14.   Isaac Watts and John B. Dykes, "Come, Holy Spirit, Heavenly Dove"

15.   Thomas Kelly and William H. Monk, "Look, Ye Saints! the Sight Is Glorious"

16.   Edward Mote and William B. Bradbury, "The Solid Rock"

17.   George Duffield and George J. Webb, "Stand Up for Jesus"

18.   Martin Luther, "A Mighty Fortress Is Our God"

19. Katharina VonSchlegel, "Be Still, My Soul"

20. William D. Longstaff and George C. Stebbins, "Take Time to Be Holy"

21. Palmer Hartsough and James H. Fillmore, "I Am Resolved"

22. William H. Bathurst and William H. Havergal, "O for a Faith That Will Not Shrink"

23. Thomas O. Chisholm and William J. Kirkpatrick, "O to be Like Thee!"

24. Charles Wesley and Carl G. Glaser, "O for a Thousand Tongues"

25. Albert B. Simpson and Mary L. Stocks, "What Will You Do with Jesus?"

26. Charles Wesley and William B. Bradbury, "Depth of Mercy"

27. Charles C. Luther and George C. Stebbins, "Must I Go, and Empty-Handed?"

28. Kenry and Melody Van Dyke from Ninth Symphony by Ludwig Von Beethoven, "Joyful, Joyful, We Adore Thee"

29. James G. Small and George C. Stebbins, "I've Found a Friend"

30. Sabine Baring-Gould and Arthur S. Sullivan, "Onward, Christian Soldiers"

31. Author Unknown, "Sitting at the Feet of Jesus"

32. Charles Wesley and George J. Elvey, "Soldiers of Christ, Arise"

33. Edwin Hatch and Robert Jackson, "Breathe on Me, Breath of God"

34. Mary Ann Thomson and James Walch, "O Zion, Haste"

35. Joseph Scriven and Charles C. Converse, "What a Friend We Have in Jesus"

36. Judson Van De Venter and Winfield S. Weeden, "I Surrender All"

37. Clara Tear Williams and Ralph E. Hudson, "Satisfied"

38. Robert Lowry, "Nothing But the Blood"

39. Johnson Oatman Jr. and Charles H. Gabriel, "Higher Ground"

40. John S. B. Monsell and William Boyd, "Fight the Good Fight"

41. Cecil F. Alexander and William H. Jude, "Jesus Calls Us"

42. Elvina M. Hall and John T. Grape, "Jesus Paid It All"

43. Annie L. Coghill and Lowell Mason, "Work, for the Night Is Coming"

44. Henry F. Lyte (Ps. 103) and Thomas Hastings, "Praise, My Soul, the King of Heaven"

45. Franklin Mason North and Gardiner's Sacred Melodies, "Where Cross the Crowded Ways of Life"

46. Martin Luther, "A Mighty Fortress Is Our God"

47. George W. Bethune and William B. Bradbury, "There Is No Name So Sweet on Earth"

48. Fanny Crosby and John R. Sweney, "Tell Me the Story of Jesus"

49. Emily E. S. Elliott and Timothy R. Matthews, "Thou Didst Leave Thy Throne"

50. Thomas Kelly and German Melody, "Praise the Savior"

51. Ralph E. Hudson and C. R. Dunbar, "I'll Live for Him"

52. William O. Cushing and Robert Lowry, "Follow On"

53. Philip P. Bliss, "Hallelujah, 'Tis Done!"

54. Frances R. Havergal and Philip P. Bliss, "I Gave My Life for Thee"

55. Charles Wesley and Lowell Mason, "A Charge to Keep I Have"

56. Edward Perronet and Oliver Holden, "All Hail the Power"

57. Henry F. Lyte and William Monk, "Abide with Me"

58. Charles Wesle, and John Zundel, "Love Divine"

59. Reginald Heber and John B. Dykes, "Holy, Holy, Holy"

60. Frances R. Havergal and James Mountain, "Like a River Glorious"

61. John Greenleaf Whittier and William V. Wallace, "Immortal Love—Forever Full"

62. Judson W. Van De Venter and Winfield S. Weeden, "Sunlight"

63. John H. Yates and Ira D. Sankey, "Faith Is the Victory"

64. Elisha A. Hoffman, "I Must Tell Jesus"

65. Matthew Bridges, Godfrey Thring, and George J. Elvey, "Crown Him with Many Crowns"

66. Mary Ann Lathbury and William F. Sherwin, "Break Thou the Bread of Life"

67. Fanny Crosby and Phoebe P. Knapp, "Blessed Assurance"

68. Carrie E. Breck and Grant Colfax Tullar, "Face to Face"

69. Charles H. Gabriel, "My Savior's Love"

70. Washington Gladden and H. Percy-Smith, "O Master, Let Me Walk with Thee"

71. Eliza E. Hewitt and Emily D. Wilson, "When We All Get to Heaven"

72. Fanny J. Crosby and John R. Sweney, "Unsearchable Riches"

73. William D. Longstaff and George C. Stebbins, "Take Time to Be Holy"

74. Wade Robinson and James Mountain, "I Am His and He Is Mine"

75. Philip P. Bliss, "Wonderful Words of Life"

76. William T. Sleeper and George C. Stebbins, "Jesus, I Come"

77. Isaac Watts and the *Gesangbuch der Herzogl,* "I Sing the Mighty Power of God"

78. Ibid.

79. Augustus M. Toplady and Thomas Hastings, "Rock of Ages"

80. Johnson Oatman Jr. and Charles H. Gabriel, "Higher Ground"

81. John S. B. Monsell and William Boyd, "Fight the Good Fight"

82. Horatius Bonar and John B. Dykes, "I Heard the Voice of Jesus Say"

83. Mary Ann Lathbury and William F. Sherwin, "Break Thou the Bread of Life"

84. Edwin Hodder and Gottfried W. Fink, "Thy Word Is Like a Garden, Lord"

85. Harper G. Smyth, "Make Me a Channel of Blessing"

86. Charles Wesley and Louis Spohr, "I Want a Principle Within"

87. Robert Lowry, "Christ Arose"

88. Lidie H. Edmunds and Norwegian Melody, "My Faith Has Found a Resting Place"

89. George Croly and Frederick C. Atkinson, "Spirit of God, Descend upon My Heart"

90. Ray Palmer and Lowell Mason, "My Faith Looks Up to Thee"

91. Elizabeth C. Clephane and Frederick C. Maker, "Beneath the Cross of Jesus"

92. Albert B. Simpson and Mary L. Stocks, "What Will You Do with Jesus?"

93. Samuel J. Stone and Samuel S. Wesley, "The Church's One Foundation"

94. Kelso R. Carter, "Standing on the Promises"

95. Frances R. Havergal and C. Luise Reichardt, "Who Is on the Lord's Side"

96. Lydia Baxter and William H. Doane, "Take the Name of Jesus with You"

97. "K"—in Rippon's *Selection of Hymns*, 1787, and Caldwell's *Union Harmony*, 1837, "How Firm a Foundation"

98. Howard A. Walter and Joseph Yates Peek, "I Would Be True"

99. George Heath and Lowell Mason, "My Soul, Be on Thy Guard"

100. John H. Yates and Ira D. Sankey, "Faith Is the Victory"

Topical Index

For further information on
audiotapes, books, and videos by Dr. Walter Martin,
as well as current seminars offered by the
Religious InfoNet, please contact:

Jill Martin Rische

Walter Martin's **Religious InfoNet**
P.O. Box 25710
St. Paul, Minnesota 55125
651-731-8040
or
Visit us at our Website!

www.waltermartin.com